Best Easy Day Hikes
Hudson River Valley

Help Us Keep This Guide Up to Date

Every effort has been made by the author and editors to make this guide as accurate and useful as possible. However, many things can change after a guide is published—trails are rerouted, regulations change, facilities come under new management, etc.

We would appreciate hearing from you concerning your experiences with this guide and how you feel it could be improved and kept up to date. While we may not be able to respond to all comments and suggestions, we'll take them to heart and we'll also make certain to share them with the author. Please send your comments and suggestions to the following address:

> GPP
> Reader Response/Editorial Department
> P.O. Box 480
> Guilford, CT 06437

Or you may e-mail us at:

> editorial@GlobePequot.com

Thanks for your input, and happy trails!

Best Easy Day Hikes Series

Best Easy Day Hikes
Hudson River Valley

Randi Minetor

FALCONGUIDES

GUILFORD, CONNECTICUT
HELENA, MONTANA
AN IMPRINT OF GLOBE PEQUOT PRESS

To buy books in quantity for corporate use
or incentives, call **(800) 962–0973**
or e-mail **premiums@GlobePequot.com**.

FALCONGUIDES®

FalconGuides is an imprint of Globe Pequot Press.

Falcon, FalconGuides, and Outfit Your Mind are registered trademarks of Morris Book Publishing, LLC.

TOPO! Explorer software and SuperQuad source maps courtesy of National Geographic Maps. For information about TOPO! Explorer, TOPO!, and Nat Geo Maps products, go to www.topo.com or www.natgeomaps.com.

Maps created by Off Route Inc. © Morris Book Publishing, LLC

Project editor: David Legere
Layout artist: Kevin Mak

Library of Congress Cataloging-in-Publication Data is available on file.

ISBN 978-0-7627-5545-5

Printed in the United States of America

10 9 8 7 6 5 4 3 2 1

Contents

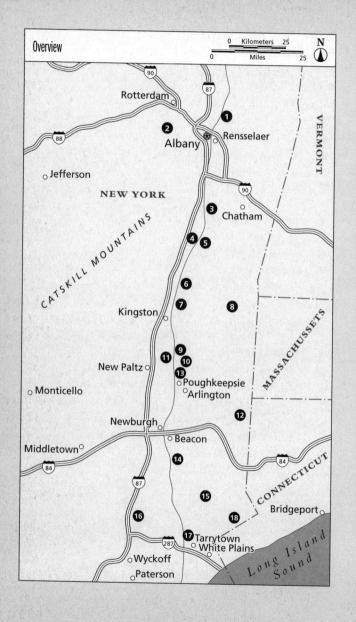

0 Kilometers 25

0 Miles 25

N

90

87

Rotterdam

88

1

2

Rensselaer

Albany

VERMONT

Jefferson

NEW YORK

90

3 Chatham

4 5

CATSKILL MOUNTAINS

6

7

8

Kingston

9

11

10

13

New Paltz

MASSACHUSSETS

Monticello

Poughkeepsie

Arlington

12

Newburgh

Middletown

Beacon

14

84

84

15

CONNECTICUT

16

87

18

Bridgeport

17 Tarrytown

287

White Plains

Wyckoff

Paterson

Long Island Sound

Acknowledgments

First, Nic and I could not be more grateful to the people who put up with our annual intrusions on their homes while we research and photograph the hikes for our books. Dan O'Donnell and Donna Tuttle opened their home to us in the Upper Hudson Valley, and Ken Horowitz and Rose-Anne Moore did the same in the Lower Hudson Valley. Without these kind, generous friends we could not take on these wonderful projects.

Writing and shooting photos for a book are only the first steps in the process; for the rest, we thank Jess Haberman, David Legere, and the creative staff at FalconGuides for their intelligent, diligent work in making all of our Best Easy Day Hikes guides successful. Likewise, we humbly thank our agent, Regina Ryan, for all that she does to keep us and our book career heading in the right direction.

Many park, preserve, and trail managers provided their time and interest in reviewing chapters of this book. In particular, we thank Linda McLean at Olana State Historic Site, Reed Sparling at Scenic Hudson, Inc., Tom Anderson at the Westchester Land Trust, Steve Oaks at Old Croton Aqueduct State Historic Park, Rod Christie with Mianus River Gorge, and Eric Lind at Constitution Marsh Audubon Center.

At home, Martin Winter continues to keep our house safe and in fine working order as we traipse about the state. We thank him and all of our friends in Rochester and beyond for their encouragement, interest, and unflagging good humor.

Finally, to the thousands of people who participated in saving the Hudson River from near-certain disaster, and to those who continue to protect it today, our hats are off to you for your extraordinary vision and your tireless dedication. Thank you for setting such a fine example for the rest of the nation to embrace and follow!

Introduction

In a region dominated by rolling green mountains, a river more than a mile wide, and a glacially sculpted landscape with prominent outcroppings of solid granite . . . can there truly be easy day hikes?

There absolutely can, and these hikes reveal some of the area's most amazing landscapes: sparkling views of a ribbon of water gliding through the valley; open vistas of mountains covered in emerald forests; and marshes, glades, and glens hidden beyond the roads. The uninformed resident or visitor might never discover these remarkable rambles into country only lightly explored—but you will, and your adventures will reveal perspectives on the Hudson River Valley you may not have thought possible.

Once the exclusive property of the very rich or the very industrial, the landscape that borders the Hudson River is now accessible to virtually anyone—and the once-troubled waterway now flows brightly, the result of the nation's first major action for resource conservation and protection of natural lands.

"Nature has spread for us a rich and delightful banquet," artist Thomas Cole once wrote of the river that inspired the first truly American style of landscape painting. "Shall we turn from it? We are still in Eden; the wall that shuts us out of the garden is our own ignorance and folly."

Cole's words were prophetic; the Hudson River struggled to survive for nearly two centuries, attacked first by the lumber industry that stripped its watershed bare, filling the river with silt and curtailing its ability to regulate its own water level. Railroad construction ordered the blasting of high cliffs in the Palisades at the Hudson's southern end, plans were revealed to use mountains for pump stations and a prison, entire cities dumped their sewage into this waterway, and major corporations chose the Hudson River as the dumping ground for toxic chemicals. As recently as the 1970s, the Hudson topped the list of endangered rivers in the United States.

Even with so much misuse in progress, the efforts to save the Hudson began all the way back in the late nineteenth century. The Hudson River's grand landscape had attracted some of the richest families in America to build castles and mansions here, and their love of the natural surroundings they called home prompted them to invest in this area, buying up endangered forests, mountains, and cliffs and turning them into state parks and wildlife refuges. The fight to cleanse the river continued throughout the 1900s, culminating in landmark legislation that catapulted environmentalism into the public consciousness. Today, industry and rampant development no longer threaten the stunning scenery, and new forests have grown where some of the old-growth woods were harvested. It's good news for the Hudson, and it's great news for day hikers and their families.

The hikes presented highlight many different facets of the Hudson, from landscapes infused with river magic rendered by painters, authors, and poets to the natural processes that allow the Hudson to regulate its own flow and cleanse its own waters. You will see the river from high above and from water level, explore its tidal marshes and its tributaries, and discover industrial passages transformed into trails that delight adults and children alike. Each provides at least a sample of the pleasures of hiking in the Hudson River Valley for people of any skill level. If you prefer hikes with more challenge, I can promise that there are many of these nearby, often in the same parks described in these pages.

When you explore the Hudson River Valley on foot, you catch a glimpse of a distant past and a vital present day. Thanks to thousands of enlightened individuals who came before us, you also see a future in which these preserved lands and the ribbon of river retain their splendor for many generations to come.

Weather

Few places can match New York State for its gorgeous spring and summer, when flower fragrances scent the air, leaves lace the trees with intense emerald shades, and the sky turns cobalt to complement the sunlight.

The sun shines six days out of ten from June through August, and while spring temperatures can linger in the 50s and 60s until June, idyllic summer days average in the 70s and 80s, with occasional spikes into the 90s in June or July, and cooler temperatures at night. Heavy rains often arrive in April, although they rarely last more than a day or two at a time. The Hudson River Valley has no dry season, so be prepared for rain any time you visit.

To truly appreciate the transformation to Technicolor spring and summer seasons in upstate New York, however, we must face the area's legendary winters. Winter temperatures average in the mid-20s, with significant dips into the teens in January, February, and March. Check the "wind chill" before making a winter hike—especially at altitude—as the air can feel much colder than the temperature indicates. The annual February thaw can push temperatures into the 50s for a few days, but the cold will return, usually lasting into mid-April. Snow is guaranteed—an average winter sees about 63 inches, although not all at once. The Hudson Valley area enjoys a high percentage of sunny days—as much as 67 percent in summer, and nearly 40 percent even in the doldrums of winter.

Fall equals spring in its spectacle, with days in the 50s and 60s, bright blue skies, and foliage panoramas all along the river and throughout the area's parks and preserves.

Park and Preserve Regulations

You will find the lands listed in this book both accessible and fairly easy to navigate. Only a few of the state parks charge admission fees (though some preserves suggest a donation).

While some of the parks have picnic areas with trash receptacles, most of the parks, forests, and preserves are "carry-in, carry-out" areas. This means that you must take all of your trash with you for disposal outside of the park. Glass containers are not permitted in any of the parks.

In all cases, dogs and other pets must be leashed—and check before you bring your puppy, because many preserves do not permit pets. You will see dogs running free in some parks, but park regulations and county leash laws prohibit this. It's also illegal to leave your dog's droppings in the park; you can face fines for not cleaning up after your pet.

Hunting is permitted on properties managed by the New York State Department of Environmental Conservation, so it's good to wear an orange jacket and hat if you're planning to hike these areas during hunting seasons.

Safety and Preparation

There is little to fear when hiking in upstate New York, whether you're climbing to summits in Harriman State Park or traversing the Old Croton Aqueduct Trail. Some basic safety precautions and intelligent preparation will make all of your hikes calamity free.

- **Wear proper footwear**. Higher boots that offer ankle support are highly recommended for all but the Walkway Over the Hudson, as most hikes in this area involve rocky terrain. A good, correctly fitted pair of hiking shoes or boots can make all the difference on a daylong hike, or even on a short walk. Look for socks that wick away moisture, or add sock liners to your footwear system.

- **Carry a first aid kit** to deal with blisters, cuts and scrapes, and insect bites and stings. Insects abound in late spring and summer in central New York, especially near wetlands, ponds, lakes, and creeks, so wear insect repellent and carry after-bite ointment or cream to apply to itchy spots. Poison ivy lines many of these trails, so watch for "leaves of three" and carry a product that is designed to remove urushiol (the oil in poison ivy) from your skin. Ask your pharmacist for recommendations.

- **Carry water**. Don't try drinking from the rivers, creeks, ponds, or other bodies of water unless you can filter or treat the water first. Your best bet is to carry your own—at least a quart for any hike, and up to a gallon in hot weather.

- **Dress in layers**, no matter what the season. If you're a vigorous hiker, you'll want to peel off a layer or two even in the dead of winter. On a summer evening, the air can cool suddenly after sunset, and rain clouds can erupt with little preamble.

- **Bring your mobile phone**. All but the most remote trails have mobile coverage, so if you do get into a jam, help is a phone call away. (Set it to vibrate while you're on trail, however, as a courtesy to the rest of us.)

- **Leave wildlife alone.** Rattlesnakes are a possibility, particularly in Harriman State Park; the snakes are generally less interested in encountering you than you are in seeing them, so sightings are rare. Black-bear sightings do happen occasionally, especially in mountain-pass areas and in state parks that border the Adirondacks and Catskills. As a general rule, don't approach wildlife of any kind. If you do see a bear, don't go closer to it; if your presence changes its behavior, you're too close. Keep your distance and the bear will most likely do the same. Some cases of rabies in raccoons have been reported in the area; generally, it's best to steer clear of these animals when they're seen in daylight.

- **Check for ticks.** Deer ticks in this area carry Lyme disease. If a tick bites you and embeds itself in your skin, don't panic—the Albany County Department of Health notes that it takes twenty-four to thirty-six hours for the tick to transfer Lyme disease to you. Remove the tick with tweezers (don't touch it with your hands), and watch for three to thirty days to see if a rash develops. You'll find more information on safe methods for deer tick removal at www.albanycounty .com/departments/health/.

Zero Impact

Trails in the Hudson River Valley and neighboring mountains are heavily used year-round. We, as trail users and advocates, must be especially vigilant to make sure our passage leaves no lasting mark. Here are some basic guidelines for preserving trails in the region:

- Pack out all your own trash, including biodegradable items like orange peels. You might also pack out garbage left by less considerate hikers.

- Don't approach or feed any wild creatures—the ground squirrel eyeing your snack food is best able to survive if it remains self-reliant.

- Don't pick wildflowers or gather rocks, antlers, feathers, and other treasures along the trail. Removing these items will only take away from the next hiker's experience.

- Avoid damaging trailside soils and plants by remaining on the established route. This is also a good rule of thumb for avoiding poison ivy, a common regional trailside irritant.

- Don't cut switchbacks, which can promote erosion.

- Be courteous by not making loud noises while hiking.

- Many of these trails are multiuse, which means you'll share them with other hikers, trail runners, mountain bikers, and equestrians. Familiarize yourself with the proper trail etiquette, yielding the trail when appropriate.

- Use outhouses at trailheads or along the trail.

Land Management

The following government and private organizations manage most of the public lands described in this guide and can provide further information on these hikes and other trails in their service areas.

- New York State Department of Parks, Recreation and Historic Preservation, Empire State Plaza, Agency Building 1, Albany 12238; (518) 474-0456; nysparks .state.ny.us. A complete listing of state parks is available on the website, along with park brochures and maps.

- The Nature Conservancy, Eastern New York Conservation Office, 195 New Karner Rd., Suite 201, Albany 12205; (518) 690-7878; www.nature.org/wherewe work/northamerica/states/newyork/preserves/art13628 .html

- Westchester Land Trust, 403 Harris Rd., Bedford Hills 10507; (914) 241-6346; www.westchesterlandtrust.org

- New York State Department of Environmental Conservation, Region 3, 21 South Putt Corners Rd., New Paltz 12561; (845) 256-3000; www.dec.ny.gov

- Appalachian National Scenic Trail, P.O. Box 50, Harpers Ferry, WV 25425; (304) 535-6278; www.nps.gov/ appa

- Friends of the Old Croton Aqueduct; (914) 693-5259; www.aqueduct.org

- Scenic Hudson, One Civic Center Plaza Suite 200, Poughkeepsie 12601; (845) 473-4440; www.scenic hudson.org

Public Transportation

The Metro-North Railroad has stops along the Hudson River as far north as Poughkeepsie, and many of the stations are close to trailheads described in this book. For complete maps and schedule information, visit www.mta.info or your nearest Metro-North station (the MTA does not publish a telephone number for general customer information).

How to Use This Guide

This guide is designed to be simple and easy to use. Each hike is described with a map and summary information that delivers the trail's vital statistics including length, difficulty, fees and permits, park hours, canine compatibility, and trail contacts. Directions to the trailhead are also provided, along with a general description of what you'll see along the way. A detailed route finder (Miles and Directions) sets forth mileages between significant landmarks along the trail.

Hike Selection

This guide describes trails that are accessible to every hiker, whether you're visiting from out of town or you are lucky enough to live in the Hudson River Valley. The hikes are no longer than 7.2 miles round-trip, and some are considerably shorter. They range in difficulty from flat excursions perfect for a family outing to a more challenging trek in the Hudson Highlands. While these trails are among the best, keep in mind that nearby trails, often in the same park or preserve, may offer options better suited to your needs. I've sought to space hikes all along the length of the river, so wherever your starting point, you'll find a great easy day hike nearby.

Difficulty Ratings

These are all easy hikes, but *easy* is a relative term. Some would argue that no hike involving any kind of climbing is easy, but the Hudson River Valley's terrain features everything from gradual slopes to mountain peaks. To aid in the selection of a hike that suits particular needs and abilities, each is rated easy, moderate, or more challenging. Bear in mind that even most challenging routes can be made easy by hiking within your limits and taking rests when you need them.

- **Easy** hikes are generally short and flat, taking no longer than an hour to complete.

- **Moderate** hikes involve increased distance and relatively mild changes in elevation, and will take one to two hours to complete.

- **More challenging** hikes feature some steep stretches, greater distances, and generally take longer than two hours to complete.

These are completely subjective ratings—consider that what you think is easy is entirely dependent on your level of fitness and the adequacy of your gear (primarily shoes). If you are hiking with a group, you should select a hike with a rating that's appropriate for the least fit and prepared in your party.

Approximate hiking times are based on the assumption that on flat ground, most walkers average two miles per hour. Adjust that rate by the steepness of the terrain and your level of fitness (subtract time if you're an aerobic animal and add time if you're hiking with kids), and you have a ballpark hiking duration. Be sure to add more time if you plan to picnic or take part in other activities like bird watching or photography.

Trail Finder

Map Legend

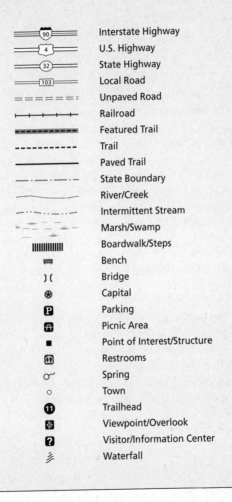

	Interstate Highway
	U.S. Highway
	State Highway
	Local Road
	Unpaved Road
	Railroad
	Featured Trail
	Trail
	Paved Trail
	State Boundary
	River/Creek
	Intermittent Stream
	Marsh/Swamp
	Boardwalk/Steps
	Bench
)(	Bridge
⊛	Capital
P	Parking
🏕	Picnic Area
■	Point of Interest/Structure
🚻	Restrooms
o⌐	Spring
o	Town
⓫	Trailhead
🗾	Viewpoint/Overlook
?	Visitor/Information Center
≋	Waterfall

1 Peebles Island State Park

Spacious water views surround this island where the Mohawk and Hudson Rivers meet, popping up from every angle as you walk the perimeter trail.

Distance: 2-mile lollipop
Approximate hiking time: 1 hour
Difficulty: Easy
Trail surface: Dirt and mowed grass path
Best season: Apr–Oct
Other trail users: Trail runners, cross-country skiers
Canine compatibility: Dogs permitted on leash
Fees and permits: Vehicle fee on weekends and holidays May–Oct; all other times free

Schedule: Open daily 7:30 a.m. to sunset
Maps: Available at the park visitor center (open Wed–Sun)
Water availability: Restrooms in visitor center
Trail contact: Peebles Island State Park, P.O. Box 295, Waterford 12188; (518) 237-7000; http://nysparks.state.ny.us/ parks/111/details.aspx

Finding the trailhead: From I-90, take exit 6A (I-787 north) to Cohoes. Continue on I-787 as it becomes NY 787. At the fourth traffic light, turn right onto Ontario Street (NY 470). Just before the Hudson River bridge to Troy, turn left on Delaware Avenue. The bridge to Peebles Island is at the end of Delaware Avenue. Park at the north end of the parking lot, past the Bleachery Complex. The trail begins on a crushed gravel path at N42 47.098' / W73 40.852'.

The Hike

Steeped in industrial history but most popular for its terrific views of the Mohawk and Hudson Rivers, Peebles

Island is a favorite hiking ground for residents of Troy and the smaller towns north of Albany. It's no wonder that this place draws visitors at any time of day and in every season: A wilderness on the edge of a formerly major manufacturing district, the island offers 191 acres of respite from the largely commercialized areas that surround it.

You won't be able to miss the former Cluett, Peabody & Company Powerhouse as you enter the park. Now serving as the park's visitor center, as well as the headquarters for the Erie Canalway National Heritage Corridor, this turn-of-the-twentieth-century edifice housed the Bleachery Complex for the company that supplied manufacturing services to Arrow Shirt Company. Cluett, Peabody & Company was the principal maker of the famous Arrow collars—detachable shirt collars that became iconic as a wardrobe staple for the common man in the 1910s and 1920s. Brilliant advertising turned Cluett, Peabody into the most successful company in the United States in the 1920s, turning out four million collars a week. The company continued to function here until 1972; you can learn more by visiting the building and seeing the extensive interpretive displays in the visitor center.

The Bleachery quickly disappears as you begin your hike. In just a few steps, the dense woods lead you to high bluffs over the Mohawk River, where the town of Waterford is visible just across the water. As the path continues, a series of islands comes into view: Bock, Goat, and Second Island appear on the west side of Peebles Island, along with one of the many dams built to prevent major flooding in central New York's numerous wet seasons.

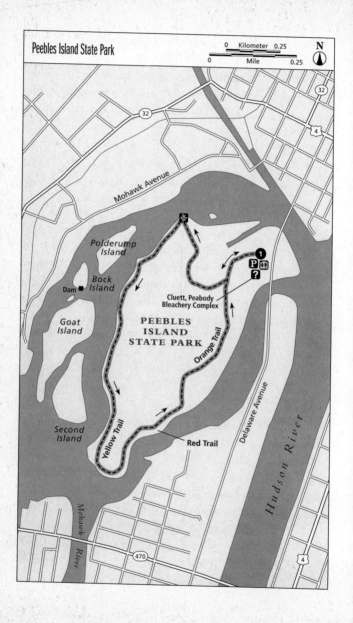

Peebles Island State Park

0   Kilometer   0.25

0   Mile   0.25

N

Mohawk Avenue

Polderump Island

Bock Island

Dam

Goat Island

Cluett, Peabody Bleachery Complex

PEEBLES ISLAND STATE PARK

Orange Trail

P

1

Delaware Avenue

Hudson River

Second Island

Yellow Trail

Red Trail

Mohawk River

470

4

32

4

At the south end of the island, you can view the split the island forms in the river; soon rocky shoals appear as you walk north on the island's east side. The uneven, sedimentary rock-strewn riverbed creates a stretch of rushing whitewater here in late winter and spring.

Miles and Directions

0.0 From the parking area, walk west on the crushed gravel path. Watch along the trail for groundhogs living in the generous understory as you approach the woods, and for deer in just about any area along the trail.

0.2 Bear right at the fork in the trail, and enter Oak Grove. Continue to bear right as the trail splinters twice more.

0.3 A side path goes to the right. Take this path to reach a great view of the river; it will rejoin the main path shortly.

0.5 This point on the island provides the first wide-open view of the water. Soon this side trail rejoins the main trail. Continue straight. You can see the town of Waterford across the river, and Bock Island is coming into view on the left.

0.6 A trail marked with red plastic disks goes left. There's a little pavilion here. Continue straight, and bear right ahead for another terrific view of the river. The dam is to the left, and Bock Island is now straight ahead. Goat Island is past the dam to the left.

0.7 You're now parallel to the dam. Second Island is coming into view.

1.2 Continue straight on the Yellow Trail. The red trail goes left. You're now rounding the southernmost part of the island.

1.3 A rocky area in the river creates a short falling-water phenomenon, with accompanying rapids.

1.4 The Yellow Trail goes left here, while the Red goes right. Take the Red Trail to the right to stay on the island's perimeter.

1.7 Turn right on the mowed grass path. (The Red Trail continues left.) Enter the woods.

1.8 Turn left on the Orange Trail. Shortly, emerge in a meadow that sports tall grasses and leafy plants in summer. Continue straight as you reach the paved area, and cross behind the Bleachery Complex to return to the parking lot.

2.0 You've completed the lollipop and arrived back at your vehicle.

2 John Boyd Thacher State Park: Indian Ladder Trail

Limestone cliffs, spectacular valley views, hanging gardens, jagged rock formations, and coves behind waterfalls: This is the must-see trail in the Capital region.

Distance: 1.6-mile lollipop
Approximate hiking time: 1 hour
Difficulty: Easy
Trail surface: Dirt path, some stairs
Best season: May–Oct
Other trail users: Hikers only
Canine compatibility: Dogs permitted on leash
Fees and permits: Vehicle fee on weekends and holidays only; all other times free
Schedule: May 1 through Labor Day: Open daily 8:00 a.m.–8:00 p.m. Labor Day through Nov 15: 8:00 a.m.–5:00 p.m. Closed Nov 16–Apr 30.

Maps: http://nysparks.state.ny .us/parks/attachments/Thacher-TrailMap.pdf
Water availability: Restrooms and refreshment stand near park entrance
Trail contact: Thacher State Park, 1 Hailes Cave Road, Voorheesville 12186; (518) 872-9133; http://nysparks.state.ny .us/parks/128/details.aspx
Special considerations: Some steep drop-offs and views from high places; not recommended for very young children. This hike features 110 stairs going down at its outset and 110 going up at the end of the gorge hike.

Finding the trailhead: From Voorheesville, take NY 85A (Helderberg Parkway/New Salem Road) west and south to the junction with NY 85 (New Scotland Road). Turn right on NY 85 and continue to the junction with NY 157. Turn right on NY 157 and continue to the park. The trail begins at N42 39.106' / W74 00.426'.

The Hike

Of the many excellent hiking opportunities in the greater Albany area, Indian Ladder Trail stands out as the best representation of central New York's geological story: The hike traces an edge of the Helderberg Escarpment, where the collision of continents hundreds of millions of years ago forced limestone, sandstone, and shale peaks up from the depths of the earth's bedrock. Over eons, wind and weather wore away the sharp peaks and left behind this long range of cliffs, breaking away great limestone slabs and leaving a rock wall perpendicular to the valley floor at its base.

Fast-forward to about a thousand years ago, when the Schoharie Indians came through here regularly on a path along the rock ridgeline we see today. Descending from the cliff above on makeshift ladders, the Indians followed the path behind waterfalls and over tricky rock faces, then climbed a ladder at the other end and returned to higher ground. Today, we call this the Indian Ladder Trail, but the ladders are gone—although they were in use as recently as the 1950s—and we now climb down sturdy metal staircases to gain access to the visual riches below.

Towering limestone walls, waterfalls originating above and below the trail, and overhangs that allow us to stand behind tumbling waters are just a few of the delights this trail produces. Remember to look behind you to catch the hanging gardens that spring forth when water seeps through porous rock walls, and to peer deep into holes in the rock to glimpse the origins of trickling streams. Don't be surprised if a chipmunk comes up to your shoe and waits expectantly—wildlife here seem to know that people mean food, but feeding the chipmunks or any other animals is illegal. Try not to be taken in by a striped, four-inch-high bandit.

You can walk the Indian Ladder Trail to its end, turn around and walk back on the same trail, or climb the 110 steps at the far end and return on the level trail at the rim of the cliff. The rim trail delivers the panoramic valley views and provides an easy return route if you've had enough of stairs, rocks, and ledges.

Miles and Directions

0.0 Park in the last lot at the end of the bank of parking areas. Before you begin your hike, stop here to enjoy the view of the valley below. To your right, you can see the very tall building standing parallel to four identical smaller buildings: These are all part of Empire State Plaza, the center of the Capital District in downtown Albany. The trail begins at the stone staircase to your left. Follow the aqua blazes.

0.2 Emerge from the trail along the rim in a mowed picnic area. Continue along the edge of the trail, which gives you another chance to admire the view.

0.4 At the end of the picnic area, take the stairs down. There are 110 steps in all, some metal and some stone. You'll come to a part of the staircase with a low ceiling—a natural overhang that's about 4.5 feet high. Stoop to go through it, and come out on the Talus Slope, a particularly striking area of rock formations. Go down another 11 steps into an area where water drips down the rock wall, creating hanging gardens of ferns and mosses.

0.5 You're behind Minelot Falls, under an overhang that extends the falls out in front of you. Note that there's water coming down behind you as well, pouring over the rock wall. The water wore holes in the rock over many years. It's easy to spot the wet areas, because plant life grows here wherever

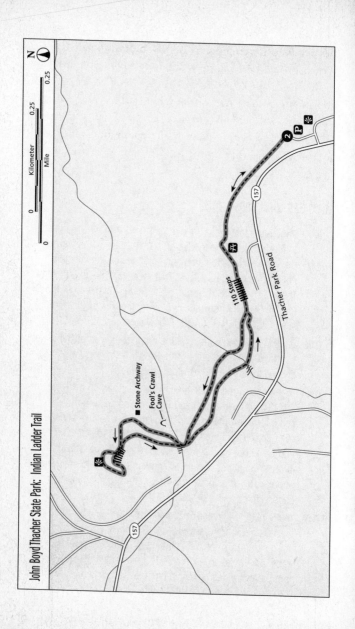

John Boyd Thacher State Park: Indian Ladder Trail

N

Kilometer
0   0.25

Mile
0   0.25

Stone Archway
Fool's Crawl
Cave

110 Steps

157

Thacher Park Road

157

2

P

there's running water. From here, cross a short boardwalk and go down eleven steps toward the second falls.

0.6 Here is the second waterfall—actually two falls, one cascading from above and one falling just in front of you. Watch your step here, as the stream that feeds this waterfall crosses the stone path here.

0.7 In this alcove, you'll find Fool's Crawl Cave, on the course of an underground stream. Look down the rocks to see this stream tumble down the cliff face.

0.8 This huge natural archway is worth exploration—there are openings for shallow caves at either side. Then continue to the staircase at the end of the path. It's sixty-two stairs up to a scenic landing, and twelve steps down from the landing to a viewing platform.

0.9 This viewing deck offers a fairly unobstructed view of the valley below—a strikingly green sight in spring and summer. When you're ready, return up these twelve steps and go up forty-eight more to return to the cliff rim. Turn left and walk back along the rim trail (still blazed aqua), and into the picnic area.

1.1 Cross this stream on stepped rocks straight ahead, or go around to your right about 100 feet to take the bridge across.

1.2 Join the paved path and continue on the bridge over the stream. The second waterfall you saw below originates here.

1.3 Steps here lead down to the path you followed on your way in, along the rim of the cliff. Take this path back to the parking area.

1.6 Here is the parking area.

3 Lewis A. Swyer Preserve

In the mood for something exotic? This boardwalk ramble takes you to a freshwater marsh and swamp that surround you with tall vegetation.

Distance: 1.2 miles out and back

Approximate hiking time: 45 minutes

Difficulty: Easy

Trail surface: Boardwalk

Best season: Apr–Nov

Other trail users: Hikers only

Canine compatibility: Pets not permitted

Fees and permits: Free

Schedule: Open daily dawn to dusk

Maps: National Geographic Topo!, New York/New Jersey edition

Water availability: None

Trail contact: The Nature Conservancy, 195 New Karner Road, Suite 200, Albany 12205; (518) 690-7850; www.nature.org/wherewework/northamerica/states/newyork/

Special considerations: Insect repellent is a must.

Finding the trailhead: From I-787 in Albany, take US 9 and 20 to Rensselaer. Turn right on NY 9J and continue 7.7 miles through Castleton. Watch for the preserve's small parking area along the road to the right (west side), about half a mile after you go under a railroad pass. The trailhead is about 500 feet south of the parking area as you reach Mill Creek. **From the south,** take NY 9J north and pass through the flashing light in Stuyvesant Landing. The parking area is 2 miles north of the flashing light. GPS: N42 25.072' / W73 46.147'

The Hike

You may live in the Hudson River Valley your entire life without coming upon Mill Creek, a quiet tributary that penetrates the river's eastern bank near Stuyvesant Landing. Here at the edge of the Hudson, Mill Creek enjoys the ebb and flow of the tide—yes, the Atlantic Ocean's tide some 150 miles south. Salt water does not find its way this far upriver, however, so Mill Creek and its surroundings have formed a freshwater marsh and swamp, a place where water flows in and out, covering the submerged land with nutrients that nurture a distinctive and verdant ecosystem.

The preserve, acquired by the Nature Conservancy in 1989, actually formed as a result of river dredging, a process of lowering the river floor to keep the waterway deep enough for major shipping traffic. The material dredged from the riverbed ended up here, creating land at the mouth of the creek. Today the Swyer Preserve protects one of only five freshwater tidal swamps in New York State.

Here the vegetation includes tall spires of pickerelweed, which bear bright purple towers of blooms in summer. The broad leaves of arrow arum sprout from the waterlogged earth. Rice cutgrass and swamp milkweed spread their roots in the marshy land, while ash, maple, slippery elm, and oak trees shade the creek's banks and provide homes for yellow warblers, warbling vireos, gray catbirds, veeries, and wood thrushes. Watch for common yellowthroats, Virginia rail, green heron, and red-winged blackbirds among the tall grasses, and keep an eye out for snapping turtles or even a water snake.

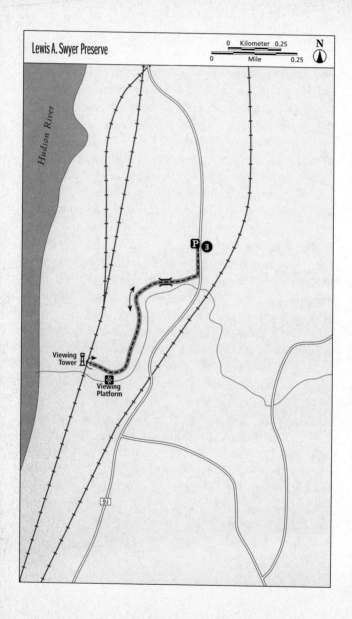

Lewis A. Swyer Preserve

0   Kilometer 0.25

0   Mile   0.25

N

Hudson River

P ❸

Viewing
Tower

Viewing
Platform

91

The short, pleasant boardwalk offers many open viewing points, with a tower at the end that provides a terrific view of the river and the passing trains on its west bank. When the tides are particularly high in spring, the water brings silt and mud up and over the boardwalk, so wear shoes that provide a good grip on a wet, slippery surface.

Miles and Directions

0.0 Park here and walk south 500 feet to the trailhead.

0.2 At the preserve sign, turn right onto the boardwalk. Stop at the kiosk, where you'll find tide tables and other useful information. In a few steps you'll come to a viewing platform, which provides a long view of the creek. Note all of the large, broad-leaved vegetation here. Shortly you'll cross a bridge.

0.6 Here is another platform, with an open view of the creek and surrounding woods. There are benches here. Watch for snails, listen for spring peepers in April and May, and see if you can hear or spot a pileated woodpecker. Just around the next bend, the boardwalk ends at a viewing tower. It's nineteen steps to the top. When you're ready, retrace your steps to return to the parking area.

1.2 You've emerged from the trail and are back at your vehicle.

4 Cohotate Preserve

See the Hudson River up close—right at the water level—and explore 3,000 continuous feet of sand, marshes, and historic foundations at the river's edge.

Distance: 1.3-mile lollipop
Approximate hiking time: 45 minutes
Difficulty: Easy
Trail surface: Dirt path with many bridges
Best season: Mar–Nov
Other trail users: Joggers, cross-country skiers
Canine compatibility: Dogs permitted on leash
Fees and permits: Free
Schedule: Open daily dawn to dusk

Maps: USGS Hudson North
Water availability: None
Trail contact: Greene County Soil and Water Conservation District, 90-7 Greene County Office Building, Cairo 12143; (518) 622-0344; www.gcswcd.com/education/cohotate.html
Special considerations: Bring binoculars in spring and fall to spot migrating waterfowl and passerines.

Finding the trailhead: From I-87, take exit 21 toward Catskill and the Rip Van Winkle Bridge. Continue east on NY 23 to NY 385 in Catskill. Turn north on NY 385 and continue for 1.9 miles. Watch for the COHOTATE PRESERVE sign on your right before you reach Athens, NY. GPS: N42 14.756' / W73 50.586'

The Hike

This little fifty-two-acre preserve protects something you may not find anywhere else along the river: more than half a mile of unbroken reclaimed land right at the edge of the water. A former site of commercial ice production, which thrived here before refrigerators became household appliances, this land now provides respite and nourishment for migrating birds as they follow the river's natural course along the Atlantic Flyway.

Your hike circles a man-made pond, crosses at least nine streams that trickle down the hillsides during late winter snowmelt and spring rains, and rolls down to the river, where you can slow your pace, stop for a picnic at one of the tables provided, and enjoy the sights and sounds along the water.

Here you will also find the Columbia-Greene County Community College Environmental Field Station, where students study field ecology. It's not open to the public, but your Scout troop or school class can return for special youth programs at the station. Call (518) 622-3620 to learn more.

Miles and Directions

0.0 Park here and walk east from the trailhead.

0.2 At the trail intersection past the information kiosk, turn left. You'll reach a pond in about 100 feet. Bear left around the pond on the mowed path.

0.3 Here is the observation deck. Look down into the water here to see fish.

0.4 Here is a bridge. Cross over it and continue straight on the path. Follow the red diamond-shaped trail markers on the trees.

0.5 Cross a bridge over a stream. (This may be dry in summer.) In about twenty steps, you'll come to another bridge. Cross this one and continue to the observation deck ahead to your left, down a short side trail. Stop here to see the Hudson River. When you're ready, go back down the spur to the main trail.

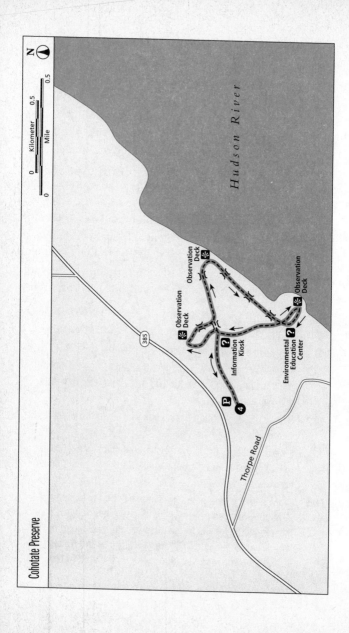

Cohotate Preserve

Hudson River

Observation Deck

Observation Deck

Information Kiosk

Environmental Education Center

Observation Deck

385

Thorpe Road

N

0   0.5   Kilometer
0   0.5   Mile

0.6 Cross another bridge. The Hudson River is on your left. From here, it's a short climb to a respectable viewpoint. Trees may obscure some of your view, but you'll be closer soon.

0.7 Cross another bridge, and make a brief, steep climb to another bridge—the sixth you've crossed so far. Rejoin the gravel path in about 100 feet. Turn left to continue the loop.

0.8 Here is the path to the Columbia-Greene County Community College Environmental Field Station. Turn left to go down to the marshy area along the river. Walk left toward the picnic area. You can see Rip Van Winkle Bridge to the north. Continue about 150 feet along the path to a little observation deck, where you can see the remains of a dock before you. This was the foundation of Empire Number Two Icehouse, where ice was once manufactured. When the ice trade ended, this and many other buildings along the Hudson were dismantled. Continue to circle the picnic area until you reach the gravel path.

1.0 Follow the gravel path uphill to the parking area. Listen for red-eyed vireos, northern cardinals, eastern phoebes, and house and purple finches in the woods as you walk.

1.1 A path to your right goes down to the water. Continue to the junction with the entrance path on your left. Turn left and return to the parking area.

1.3 Here is the parking area.

5 Olana State Historic Site

Walk in the footsteps of some of America's most celebrated artists and see the view that inspired the Hudson River School of painting.

Distance: 1.2-mile loop
Approximate hiking time: 45 minutes
Difficulty: Easy
Trail surface: Crushed shale and paved paths
Best season: Mar–Nov
Other trail users: Joggers, cross-country skiers
Canine compatibility: Dogs permitted on leash
Fees and permits: Fee for grounds access on weekends and holidays, Apr–Oct. If you prefer not to pay the fee, park in the lot at the base of the hill near the lake, and walk up the hill from there.

Schedule: Grounds are open daily 8:00 a.m to sunset
Maps: At Olana's website: www .olana.org/visit_tours.php
Water availability: At the visitor center and at the Wagon House at the lower lot
Trail contact: Olana State Historic Site, 5720 State Route 9G, Hudson 12534; (518) 828-0135; www.olana.org
Special considerations: The admission fee can be credited toward a ticket to tour the house. Reservations are recommended for house tours.

Finding the trailhead: From I-87 north or south, take exit 21 for Catskill. Follow NY 23 east to the Rip Van Winkle Bridge. Cross the bridge and bear right onto NY 9G south. Olana is 1 mile south of the bridge, on the left. The street address is 5720 State Rte. 9G in Hudson. GPS: N42 13.101' / W73 49.776'

The Hike

Watch the sun sink low over the Hudson River from the grounds of this majestic home, and you will understand how this magnificent view inspired an entirely new style of landscape painting in the mid-nineteenth century. Frederic Edwin Church (1826–1900) lived here in the castlelike mansion at Olana, and his work helped establish the American painting style that came to be known as the Hudson River School.

You may want to go inside and tour the house before taking this walk around the grounds to see some of the paintings Church produced while gazing at the river, the Catskill Mountains, and the Taconic Hills from his studio. Translating these miracles of nature to canvas, Church became one of the most celebrated artists of the Hudson River School, rising to considerable popularity during his lifetime—enough to purchase this property and build the Middle East–inspired home in which he lived with his wife and children.

The viewpoints on these grounds became the backdrop for Church's personal work of art: the 250-acre landscape he designed in an established style known as "American picturesque." (Frederick Law Olmsted, the greatest of American landscape designers, created New York's Central Park in this style.) Church established an orchard, planted thousands of trees, installed a lake, and added the carriage trails that we can walk today. Closer to the house, you can see a cutting garden created for Mrs. Church to provide cut flowers for the house.

This hike provides the complete picture—expansive views, stretches of dense forest, and opportunities to stop

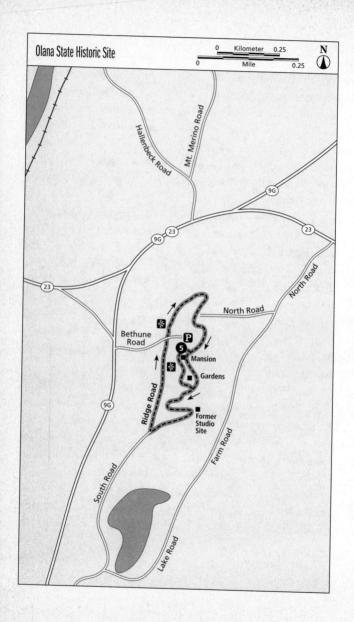

Olana State Historic Site

Kilometer 0.25
0
0   Mile   0.25

N

Hallenbeck Road

Mt. Merino Road

9G

23

9G   23

23

North Road

North Road

Bethune Road

P

5

Mansion

Gardens

Ridge Road

Former Studio Site

9G

South Road

Farm Road

Lake Road

and smell the flowers that grace the hillside closest to the Persian-style mansion above.

Miles and Directions

0.0 Park in the lot at the top of the property, nearest the house. From the parking area, take the brick stairway down to the carriage road. At the bottom, cross the road and begin walking on the carriage road.

0.1 Stop here to view the house from the outside. Bear left at the fork. The mansion is on your right as the formal garden comes into view. Depending on the season, you may see peonies, iris, black-eyed Susans, purple salvia, honeysuckle, allium, and many other plants in bloom. After the garden, the trail continues through an open meadow. Your first view of the Hudson River is directly in front of you.

0.3 As you come to the farthest bend in the carriage road, the Hudson Valley landscape opens in front of you. Even the three radio towers do not mar the extraordinary view. The carriage road turns left here.

0.4 This is the site of Church's former studio (which no longer stands). Not surprisingly, it features one of the finest views of the river and valley you've seen so far. Art historians call this "one of the most celebrated [views] in American art and landscape history." From here, continue to the road and turn right, walking along the road for a short stretch.

0.6 Turn right on the carriage road marked "Ridge Road." You'll come to a path to the left shortly; this is the route down to the main road used by the Churches and their guests. Pass this intersection and continue straight (bearing right at this fork).

0.7 An open area on the right has a marshy bottom, so you may see a significant difference in the vegetation here. This is one of the best places to view the mansion's towers.

0.8 Your walk up this gentle but steady incline is rewarded with the Hudson River view you came to Olana to see. As you walk the next level stretch, the Rip Van Winkle Bridge comes into view. Continue on the carriage road.

1.1 You can turn right here to return to the house and the parking area. If you want to go down to the lake, continue straight (bear left at fork) onto North Road. At the junction, continue around to the visitor center and house. The view from behind the house is one of the best on the property. As you walk from the house, you'll pass above the cultivated garden you saw earlier. You may want to stop here and stroll through the garden to enjoy the plantings.

1.2 Turn left to complete the loop and return to the parking area.

6 Tivoli Bays Wildlife Management Area: Overlook Trail

A bluff-top view of a freshwater tidal marsh awaits you at the end of this trail, while the route through wild, open meadows and dense woodlands reveals habitat for a wide assortment of birds, butterflies, and small furry creatures.

Distance: 2.6-mile lollipop
Approximate hiking time: 1.5 hours
Difficulty: Easy
Trail surface: Dirt and mowed grass path
Best season: Apr–Nov
Other trail users: Trail runners, cross-country skiers
Canine compatibility: Dogs permitted on leash

Fees and permits: Free
Schedule: Open daily dawn to dusk
Maps: inside.bard.edu/archaeology/tivolibays/map_large.html
Water availability: None
Trail contact: NYS Dept of Environmental Conservation, Norrie Point Environmental Center, P.O. Box 315, Staartsburg 12580; (845) 758-7010; www.dec.ny.gov

Finding the trailhead: From I-87, take exit 19 toward Kingston and the Rhinecliff Bridge. At the traffic circle, take the first exit onto NY 28 north. Merge onto US 209 north, and continue on US 209 for 3.8 miles. Stay on this road as it becomes NY 199, and cross the Rhinecliff Bridge. Turn left at the junction with NY 9G. Continue 4.5 miles to the parking area for Tivoli Bays Wildlife Management Area, on your left. GPS: N42 02.167' / W73 53.741'

The Hike

It may surprise you that the Hudson River is affected by the Atlantic Ocean tides, but the ebb and flow that reach

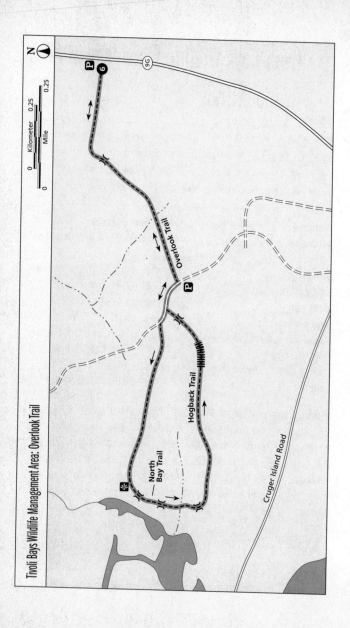

Tivoli Bays Wildlife Management Area: Overlook Trail

N

Kilometer
0   0.25
Mile
0   0.25

9G

P

P

Overlook Trail

Hogback Trail

North
Bay Trail

Cruger Island Road

the river's mouth in Long Island Sound have an influence upriver all the way to the Federal Dam in Troy. The complex ecosystem is known as the Hudson River Estuary, and one of the best places to see how its tides create a freshwater marsh is at the end of this trail.

Here the Tivoli Bays are miraculously safe from development, thanks to the work of the Hudson River National Estuarine Research Reserve, which uses this area as a field research center. The state's Department of Environmental Conservation oversees protection of the land we cross on this hike, for the good of the wildlife that thrives in this area.

And what exciting wildlife it is! Blue-winged warblers call from vine-covered trees in the middle of meadows; pileated woodpeckers announce their presence as they excavate new cavities in dead trees; red admiral butterflies dart from one blossom to the next. Vireos, warblers, thrushes, jays, and orioles pause here on their way to breeding grounds farther north or remain to repopulate their species right here, where abundant natural food is within easy reach of nest sites. A trail of bluebird boxes erupt with tiny peeps as busy eastern bluebirds fly off to forage for food and return to their nestlings with full bills. Marsh wrens fill the air with their chatter as you reach the overlook, and careful observers may spot a Virginia rail or least bittern among the cattails. In the woods, chipmunks and squirrels vie for the best food and places to store it, while signs at the parking areas note that black bears occasionally make appearances here.

Your hike begins by following the Overlook Trail (red markers) to an excellent view of Tivoli Bays, then turns onto the North Bay Trail (blue) until it reaches the Hogback Trail (yellow) for a short ascent into a drier portion of the woods. The route finally rejoins the Overlook Trail and follows it back to the parking area.

Miles and Directions

0.0 Begin at the parking lot on Route 9G. There's only one trail-head from here, leading into the woods. Follow the red plastic markers that say TRAIL or FOOT TRAIL. Cross through thick vegetation, then through a more open area.

0.2 A path goes off right. Continue straight. In about fifty steps, the red trail turns left. In a short while, cross a small bridge over a stream.

0.4 There's no bridge here, but there may be water in the stream during the snowmelt season or after heavy rains. Cross on rocks. In a few steps, cross another stream on rocks.

0.5 The trail leaves the woods and enters an open meadow. Continue across.

0.6 Merge here with a crushed stone path, and turn right.

0.7 The Hogback Trail (yellow markers) goes left here. Pass it, and turn left on the next trail, which has red markers.

1.2 Re-enter the forest, and continue to the overlook point. From here you have a view through the trees, where you can see Tivoli Bays and the many grassy islands created by the tide's rise and fall. When you're ready, turn left on the Blue Trail. Begin a fairly easy descent.

1.3 At the bridge, turn left. Cross two more bridges.

1.5 The Hogback Trail (yellow markers) goes left here. Turn left and begin a gradual ascent.

1.9 Cross a section of boardwalk. Then cross a bridge, and emerge in the meadow.

2.0 When you see the red trail markers, turn right and begin your return on the red trail. Follow this back to the parking area.

2.6 You've reached your vehicle.

7 Poets' Walk Park

Romantic, idyllic, pastoral, inspirational—this hike is all of these and more.

Distance: 2.4-mile lollipop
Approximate hiking time: 1.25 hours
Difficulty: Easy
Trail surface: Mowed and gravel paths
Best season: Apr–Nov
Other trail users: Trail runners, cross-country skiers, birders
Canine compatibility: Dogs permitted on leash
Fees and permits: Free (groups must register in advance)
Schedule: Open daily 9:00 a.m. Closing times vary with the season; check www.scenichudson .org/parks.

Maps: Scenic Hudson, www .scenichudson.org/files/u2/ PoetsWalk_webmap.jpg; Hudson Valley Network, www.hvnet.com
Water availability: None
Trail contact: Scenic Hudson, One Civic Center Plaza, Suite 200, Poughkeepsie 12601; (845) 473-4440; www.scenic hudson.org
Special considerations: People really do come here to read or write poetry; respect their desire for quiet contemplation.

Finding the trailhead: The park is located in Red Hook, Duchess County. From I-87, take exit 19 toward the Kingston-Rhinecliff Bridge. At the traffic circle, take the first exit onto NY 28 north. Merge onto US 209 north, and continue on US 209 for 3.8 miles. Stay on this road as it becomes NY 199, and cross the Kingston-Rhinecliff Bridge. Turn left onto County Route 103 (River Road). Poets' Walk Park is on the left side of the road. GPS: N41 58.846' / W73 55.239'

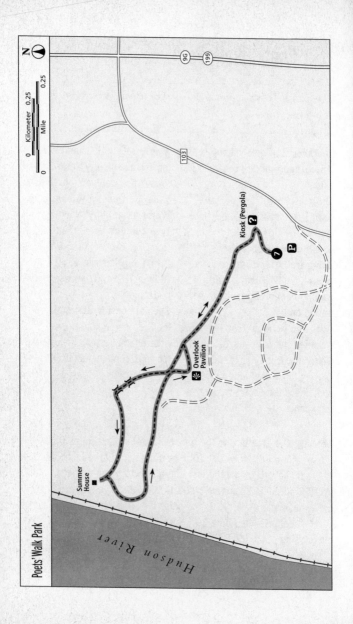

Poets' Walk Park

The Hike

If you're thinking about writing a poem, a story, or the great American novel, and you're wondering where you will ever find your Muse, you may discover your errant sprite while considering the wonders of nature in this contemplative place.

Poets' Walk began as the vision of landscape architect Hans Jacob Ehlers, who was hired by landowners Frank H. Delano and his wife, Laura Astor Delano, to improve the grounds of their estate. Inspired by the land's location and by stories of writers Washington Irving and Fitz-Green Halleck strolling here, Ehlers created the path we walk today as a connecting trail between outdoor "rooms," moving from wide views atop grassy hills to cozy sylvan glades. He intended Poets' Walk as a celebration of nature and its connection with art, and the popularity of this little linear park gives testimony to the architect's success.

You may note the lack of industrial or mercantile encroachment around the edges of this park. Scenic Hudson deserves the credit for this. It secured conservation easements on 800 acres of surrounding property, ensuring that development will not mar the pastoral atmosphere of this lovely place.

Miles and Directions

0.0 Begin the trail at the southwest end of the parking area. At the pergola, the trail continues left through a meadow filled with tall grasses and bluebird boxes.

0.5 The trail forks here; bear left. The Overlook Pavilion comes into view.

0.7 Here is the Overlook Pavilion. There's plenty of seating to allow you to enjoy the view of the Catskill Mountains. You can see the Kingston-Rhinecliff Bridge as you reach the benches to the right of the trail. Listen for bobolinks and meadowlarks singing in the grassy field, and watch for eastern bluebirds and tree swallows. When you're ready, proceed up the trail to the north; bear right toward the Summer House. Enter rolling woods of maple, beech, hickory, and other deciduous trees.

0.8 Cross a small bridge over a trickling stream (note the rough-hewn wood construction of the bridge). The trail provides a high vantage point, so you can look down into the woods—especially advantageous for seeing warblers and vireos. The trail begins to descend to a stone bridge.

1.0 Here is the stone bridge. Cross it and continue to the Summer House.

1.2 The Summer House is actually a gazebo with built-in benches. There's a great view of the Hudson River here, with the Kingston-Rhinecliff Bridge to your left. The small wetland area here is home to red-winged blackbirds, common yellowthroat, marsh wren, and other water-loving birds. The woods now include white pine and hemlock among the oak, maple, and beech trees. When you're ready, return to the trail and turn right.

1.3 Cross a bridge, and look for the interesting root patterns of trees holding their own along a river tributary. Begin a short ascent to the meadow.

1.4 At the top of the hill, there's a bench with an excellent view of the river. Watch for bald eagles here, as well as Baltimore orioles, field sparrows, and Tennessee warblers. From here, continue down the path to the southeast.

1.8 This is the intersection you encountered when you began your walk. Continue straight toward the parking area.

2.4 You've reached the parking area and your vehicle.

8 Thompson Pond

Circle a 15,000-year-old glacial kettle lake and discover a hidden wetland at the base of Stissing Mountain.

Distance: 2.6-mile loop
Approximate hiking time: 1.5 hours
Difficulty: Easy
Trail surface: Dirt paths, some boardwalk
Best season: Apr–Nov
Other trail users: Cross-country skiers, birders
Canine compatibility: No pets permitted
Fees and permits: Free
Schedule: Open daily dawn to dusk
Maps: The Nature Conservancy, www.nature.org/wherewework/ northamerica/states/newyork/ files/thompsonpond.pdf
Water availability: None; do not drink the pond water without purifying it.
Trail contact: The Nature Conservancy, 195 New Karner Rd., Suite 200, Albany 12205; (518) 690-7850; www.nature.org
Special considerations: Insect repellent is a must. Guard against ticks by wearing long pants and tucking them into your socks.

Finding the trailhead: From the Taconic Parkway, take the exit for NY 199, and travel east on NY 199 to NY 82. Follow NY 82 south to Pine Plains. Turn right on Lake Road. Continue 1.6 miles to the parking area and preserve entrance, which are on the left side of the road. GPS: N41 58.052' / W73 40.913'

The Hike

Back when North America was beginning to warm up toward the end of the last Ice Age, a massive chunk of glacial ice scooped out a depression in an area west of today's

Pine Plains. As the ice chunk melted, it filled the depression and created a sizable body of water. Time and erosion have divided this single body into Twin Island Lake, Stissing Pond, and Thompson Pond—and the Nature Conservancy protects Thompson Pond, providing us with recreational access to this unusual kettle pond and its abundance of plant and animal life.

A National Natural Landmark, Thompson Pond has more claims to fame than its glacial origin. It contains a wetland that is calcareous—it has a high concentration of calcium carbonate because of the limestone in its soil. This means that the pond and the adjacent swamp can support wildlife and plants that are not found in many other wetlands. The ferns and wildflowers you see here may seem strange and exotic, especially along the boardwalk through the swamp. Look for pipewort, marsh St. Johnswort, and unusual ferns and wildflowers. In all, 387 plant species thrive in this preserve, alongside 27 mammal species and a remarkable 162 different bird species.

Your hike follows the yellow-marked trail all the way around the pond, through forests of maple, hemlock, hickory, and ash, along cattail marshes, past open farm fields and a cattle pasture, and through areas where wildflowers crowd the understory. With its fairly remote location and its widely diverse habitats, this hike truly brings you into the wilderness for a much-needed break from civilized life.

Miles and Directions

0.0 Park along the roadside. The trail begins due south of the road. Follow the diamond-shaped green markers with yellow arrows—this is the Yellow Trail.

0.3 Stop at the kiosk to sign the trail registry. Make a quick detour by taking the Blue Trail (green markers with blue arrows) to your left for a view of the lake. Follow the Blue Trail around until it reconnects with the Yellow Trail.

0.5 Turn left as you rejoin the Yellow Trail. Now the trail is marked with yellow blazes on the trees as well as with the plastic markers.

0.6 At this intersection, the Blue Trail goes right, while the yellow goes left. Bear left on the Yellow Trail. The pond becomes more visible through the trees to your left.

0.7 A stone bench here marks a nice viewpoint.

0.8 Here's a second bench with a welcome view of the pond. From here, the trail descends for a short stretch. You may see considerable evidence of beaver activity here. Marsh wrens, yellow warblers, warbling vireos, and swamp sparrows all sing in the marsh along the pond.

1.0 The Yellow Trail goes left, while the blue goes right. Go left and continue on the Yellow Trail. Be careful not to trip into the barbed wire fence on your right. The land beyond is a private farm.

1.2 Descend a set of steps to a narrow boardwalk over the swamp. This is the most fascinating section of the hike, with the feeling of a jungle or a tropical rainforest. Trees are covered with vines, plants have extra-large leaves, tree limbs overhang the trail, and tall grasses obscure the view on either side.

1.3 The boardwalk ends. Continue through an area of dense vegetation, with a bog to your left and rolling farmland to your right. This area can be muddy; there are some lengths of two-plank boardwalk to get you through the wettest portions.

1.6 Do you hear mooing? The farmer's dairy barn comes into view on your right. The last length of boardwalk ends here. In a moment, the vegetation parts and you have a clear view of

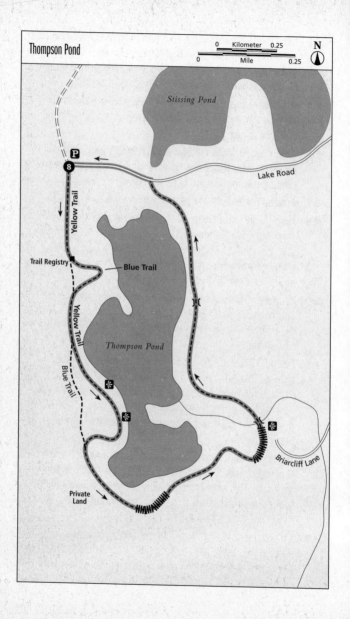

Thompson Pond

Stissing Pond

Lake Road

P
8

Yellow Trail

Trail Registry

Blue Trail

Yellow Trail

Blue Trail

Thompson Pond

Private Land

Briarcliff Lane

0   Kilometer   0.25

0   Mile   0.25

N

the pond. Tree islands grow here, with grasses at their bases and roots exposed above the water. You may see wild iris here in spring.

1.7 Cross a bridge. This is a good spot to stop and look at the tree-island area. You'll see lily pads here too, which bloom in midsummer. Re-enter the woods.

2.1 A hunting field appears on the right after the woods. Continue straight. Ahead, the grassy areas fill with dame's rocket's purple and lavender flowers in spring and other wildflowers throughout the summer. Berry vines here produce raspberries in July.

2.4 The trail ends at the road. Turn left to walk back to your car, and be sure to stop and enjoy the view of the pond as you go.

2.6 Here is the parking area.

9 Roosevelt Farm and Forest

Our nation's only four-term president left us this uncommonly lovely woodland, as well as the carriage roads that bring us to its verdant heart.

Distance: 2.7-mile lollipop
Approximate hiking time: 1.5 hours
Difficulty: Easy
Trail surface: Crushed stone, dirt, and mowed-grass path
Best season: Apr–Nov
Other trail users: Trail runners, cross-country skiers, cyclists, horseback riders
Canine compatibility: Dogs permitted on leash
Fees and permits: Walking the trail is free; there is a fee to visit the presidential library.
Schedule: Open daily sunrise to sunset

Maps: Available at the Henry A. Wallace Visitor Center at Franklin D. Roosevelt Presidential Library and Museum
Water availability: Restrooms in visitor center
Trail contact: FDR Presidential Library and Museum, 4079 Albany Post Rd., Hyde Park 12538; (800) FDR-VISIT or (845) 486-7770; www.fdrlibrary .marist.edu
Special considerations: Take precautions against ticks and poison ivy.

Finding the trailhead: **From Manhattan,** take the Henry Hudson Parkway north to the Taconic Parkway, and continue to I-84 west. Take I-84 to US 9 north. The FDR Library is on the left side of US 9, 4 miles north of Poughkeepsie, while Roosevelt Farm and Woods is on the right side of NY 9, directly across from the library. **From Albany,** take the New York State Thruway (1-87) south to exit 18 at New Paltz. Take the exit and follow NY 299 east to US 9W south. Cross the Mid-Hudson Bridge and continue to US 9 north. The FDR Library is on the left side of US 9, while Roosevelt Farm and Woods

The Hike

If you weren't around during the Great Depression or World War II, Franklin Delano Roosevelt's name may be no more to you than one in a list of forty-odd presidents of the United States. For history enthusiasts and those who lived during his four-term presidency, however, the list of Roosevelt's accomplishments extends well beyond the pages of any textbook—and one of the least known of these is his devotion to conservation, well before the environment became a fashionable cause.

We are fortunate to be able to enjoy the literal fruits of Roosevelt's land preservation efforts here at the last remaining acres of his own farm and forest, saved from development in 2004 by the Scenic Hudson Land Trust, and now preserved by the National Park Service. Just across the street, the Home of Franklin D. Roosevelt National Historic Site tells the fascinating story of the president's battle with polio, his life outside of the White House, and his relationship with his wife, the venerable First Lady Eleanor Roosevelt. The FDR Presidential Library and Museum fill in all the blanks about the successes that brought this president four terms in the White House: the establishment of Social Security, the New Deal that hastened the end of the Depression, creation of the Civilian Conservation Corps, and his leadership during World War II, to name just a few.

Somewhere in the midst of his twelve-plus years in Washington (Roosevelt died in 1945, just a few months into his fourth term), the president found the time to learn about scientific forestry, the management of a sustainable

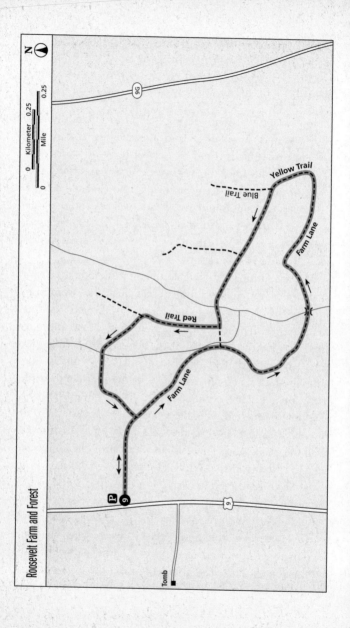

Roosevelt Farm and Forest

timber crop with a careful balance between environmental protection and harvesting. At his direction, more than half a million trees were planted on his property here in Hyde Park, creating the strikingly beautiful woodland that surrounds this trail. This mixed forest features many species that are native to the Hudson River Valley: beech, poplar, tulip tree, maple, and oak, as well as eastern hemlock and other conifers. The forest floor's carpet of ferns and many naturally occurring broadleaf plants is unusually lovely, the result of smart, health-enriching forestry practices still maintained today.

Your walk begins by following the Farm Lane, one of the many carriage roads used by the president and his family, and now open only to foot and bicycle traffic. As you near the end of this road, the route we've chosen turns and leads down two woodland trails, immersing you in the kind of forest we read about in storybooks. The trail loops back to rejoin the carriage road where you began.

Miles and Directions

0.0 Begin at the parking lot. The Farm Lane carriage trail leads east. You'll see trail markers: a white disk with a green tulip-tree leaf. Every tenth-mile, wooden markers on your left note the distance you've walked.

0.3 The Red Trail goes left here (it's marked with a wooden sign). Continue straight. In about thirty steps, a path goes right. You will see many of these unmarked paths as you walk down the carriage road.

0.6 The Yellow Trail goes off to the left here. Continue on the Farm Lane (bear right at the fork). A stream flows to your left.

0.9 Cross a bridge over a gentle stream. Just after the bridge, a side trail goes left. Continue straight.

1.4 The Yellow Trail begins to your left. Turn left onto the Yellow Trail. Follow the yellow blazes on trees, every 20 yards or so.

1.5 The Blue Trail goes right. Continue straight on the Yellow Trail. Note the eastern hemlocks in this section of the woods, lining both sides of the trail.

1.8 At the trail intersection, go left on the Yellow Trail, then left again at the second intersection (just after you cross the stream).

1.9 The Red Trail begins on your right. Turn right and follow the Red Trail. You'll see red blazes on the trees.

2.2 At the trail junction, take the left fork and continue to follow the Red Trail.

2.3 At the junction with three red blazes, turn left.

2.4 You've reached Farm Lane. Turn right on Farm Lane and return to the parking lot.

2.7 You've reached your vehicle.

10 Vanderbilt Mansion National Historic Site

See how the other one-millionth percent lived by walking in their footsteps, exploring the lush forests and scenic viewpoints of the very, very rich.

Distance: 2.4-mile loop
Approximate hiking time: 1.5 hours
Difficulty: Easy
Trail surface: Crushed stone, dirt, and some pavement
Best season: Apr–Nov
Other trail users: Trail runners, cross-country skiers, cyclists, horseback riders
Canine compatibility: Dogs permitted on leash
Fees and permits: Walking the trail is free; there is a fee to visit the mansion.
Schedule: Open daily sunrise to sunset; the mansion is open for tours 9:00 a.m.–5:00 p.m. (closed Thanksgiving, Christmas Day, New Year's Day)
Maps: Available at the visitor center
Water availability: Restrooms in visitor center
Trail contact: Vanderbilt Mansion National Historic Site, 4097 Albany Post Rd., Hyde Park 12538; (845) 229-9115; www.nps.gov/vama
Special considerations: Take precautions against ticks and poison ivy.

Finding the trailhead: From Manhattan, take the Henry Hudson Parkway north to the Taconic Parkway, and continue to I-84 west. Take I-84 to US 9 north. Vanderbilt Mansion is on the left side of US 9, 4 miles north of Poughkeepsie. **From Albany,** take the New York State Thruway (1-87) south to exit 18 at New Paltz. Take the exit and follow NY 299 east to US 9W south. Cross the Mid-Hudson Bridge and continue to US 9 north. Vanderbilt Mansion is on the left side of US 9. GPS: N41 48.121' / W73 56.465'

The Hike

Few names are as closely associated with fabulous nineteenth-century wealth as Cornelius "Commodore" Vanderbilt, the richest man in America in his day. This opulent property belonged to his grandson, Frederick Vanderbilt, who purchased it in 1895. Frederick owned the New York Central Railroad, which passed close to the estate, so he and his family knew that this spot afforded them exceptional views of the Hudson River. The property had fallen into benign neglect when the Vanderbilts acquired it, but Frederick saw the potential in the natural setting and expansive grounds, allowing his love of nature to guide him in selecting a summer home he would share with his wife and children.

The Vanderbilts spent only a few weeks here each summer and winter, but a staff of sixty people maintained the mansion and the 600-acre grounds throughout the year. Frederick himself oversaw the restoration of the gardens and grounds. He ordered the clearing of bridle trails through the woods between the mansion and the river, renovation of the formal Italian gardens, and the construction of a steel and concrete bridge over the man-made pond. Today, we have Frederick to thank for the peaceful trails, expansive views, and perennial blooms we enjoy on this hike.

This walk is part of the Hyde Park Trail, a network of hiking trails neatly linked through a partnership between the Town of Hyde Park, the National Park Service, and other organizations. More than 10 miles in length, the total trail includes Roosevelt Farm and Forest, Home of FDR National Historic Site, Eleanor Roosevelt National Historic Site, Winnakee Nature Preserve, Mills Norrie State Park, and Hackett Hill, Pinewoods, and Riverfront Parks. Find more information about this trail network at www.hyde parkny.us/Recreation/Trails/.

Miles and Directions

0.0 Begin at the parking lot to the right (north) of the mansion. The hike begins in the northwest corner of the parking area. Begin walking north on the road. The wonderful views of the river begin fairly quickly to your left as you walk.

0.1 The road goes straight and to the right. Continue straight (follow the signs for Bard Rock).

0.2 Leave the road and take the path to your left. Descend on the path and meet up with the road again. (Alternately, you can skip this shorter path and continue to walk on the road.) Follow the road down to the west, toward the river. The open field to your left is home to goldfinches, meadowlarks, tree swallows, and many other birds.

0.4 A path goes left here. This is the Hyde Park Trail; you'll come back to this shortly. For now, continue straight to see the view from Bard Rock. Cross the one-lane bridge.

0.5 Here is Bard Rock. The view of the river here is unsurpassed. (There's parking here, if you want to return with your vehicle at another time.) When you're ready, turn around and go back across the one-lane bridge to the Hyde Park Trail.

0.6 Turn right on the Hyde Park Trail, and begin walking through the woods.

1.2 Vanderbilt Mansion comes into view on the left.

1.3 The trail to the left is a shortcut to the gardens and parking area. Continue straight.

1.7 Cross the chain barrier and continue to the road. At the road, turn left (there's an exit gate to your right).

1.8 Take the trail to your left, back into the woods. Begin a short but pronounced ascent. The trail levels off shortly.

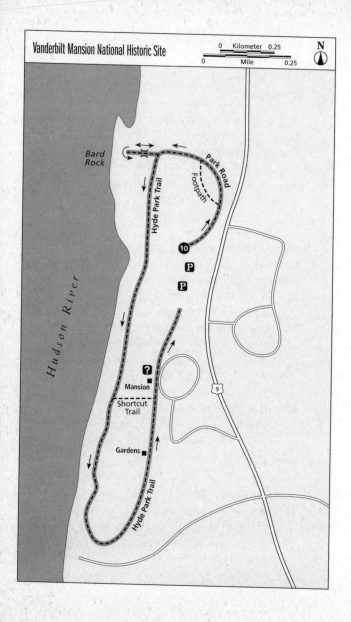

Vanderbilt Mansion National Historic Site

Kilometer 0.25
Mile 0.25

N

Bard Rock

Hudson River

Park Road

Footpath

Hyde Park Trail

10

P
P

Mansion

Shortcut Trail

Gardens

Hyde Park Trail

9

2.0 You've arrived at the Vanderbilt formal gardens. Take some time here to stroll through and enjoy the variety of shrubs and flowers.

2.2 Here is the south entrance to Vanderbilt Mansion. Bear right on the gravel path around the building. Cross the pavement and continue north on the gravel path toward the parking area.

2.3 Continue north on the sidewalk. At the visitor center, turn right and proceed to the parking lot.

2.4 You've reached the beginning of the spacious parking area. Continue across it to your vehicle.

11 Black Creek Preserve

Shady forest, vernal pools, and a dramatic suspension bridge over a dark, burbling creek—this preserve packs a lot of scenery into its 130 acres.

Distance: 1.8-mile lollipop
Approximate hiking time: 1 hour
Difficulty: Easy
Trail surface: Dirt path
Best season: Apr–Nov
Other trail users: Trail runners, cross-country skiers, cyclists, horseback riders, birders, anglers
Canine compatibility: Dogs permitted on leash
Fees and permits: Free; groups must register in advance
Schedule: Open daily dawn to dusk

Maps: Scenic Hudson Land Trust, www.scenichudson.org/files/u2/BlackCreek_webmap.jpg
Water availability: None
Trail contact: Scenic Hudson, One Civic Center Plaza, Suite 200, Poughkeepsie 12601; (845) 473-4440; www.scenichudson.org
Special considerations: Take precautions against ticks and poison ivy. Suspension bridge may be slippery in winter.

Finding the trailhead: Take I-87 to the New Paltz exit (18), and go east on NY 299 for 6 miles to the junction with US 9W. Continue north for 5.5 miles on US 9W to Winding Brook Acres Road; turn right. The parking area is on your left, just after the turn onto Winding Brook Acres Road. GPS: N41 49.209' / W73 57.820'

The Hike

Protected since 1992, Black Creek Preserve offers a network of three trails that follows the tannic acid–dyed Black Creek, wanders among vernal pools (generally visible only in spring and rainy summers), and finally leads to water-level views of the Hudson River. It's easy to see the entire preserve in a single hike, as the trails provide viewing access to virtually all of its 130 acres.

Every unspoiled acre of the Hudson River Valley deserves protection, but this preserve offers considerable natural value beyond the river's attributes. Black Creek is spawning territory for the American blue herring, and the thick forest provides cover, resting places, and food for migrating birds. Vernal pools—small, seasonal ponds that fill with water in spring but dry up in summer—are homes for small amphibians like frogs and salamanders. Keep an eye out for tiny hopping or slithering creatures as you walk the trails.

Saving land from residential or industrial development is only the first step in preserving and protecting it forever. You'll see interpretive signs here about the wooly adelgid beetle, a nasty critter that devours hemlock trees. Keeping the understory healthy throughout the forest also falls to Scenic Hudson, so you will see fences that keep the resident deer from overgrazing in some areas. Land stewardship—often performed by dedicated volunteers—makes wildlife preserves like this one such delightful refuges for the human spirit as well as for animals, birds, and native plants.

Miles and Directions

0.0 Cross the driveway from the parking area and begin the trail at the archway fashioned from tree branches. The trail begins by following Black Creek. Cross a small bridge.

0.1 Cross the suspension bridge over Black Creek, and begin to follow the yellow plastic markers you see on trees. Enter the forest and note the predominance of young hemlock trees here. As you proceed uphill—the steepest part of the trail—

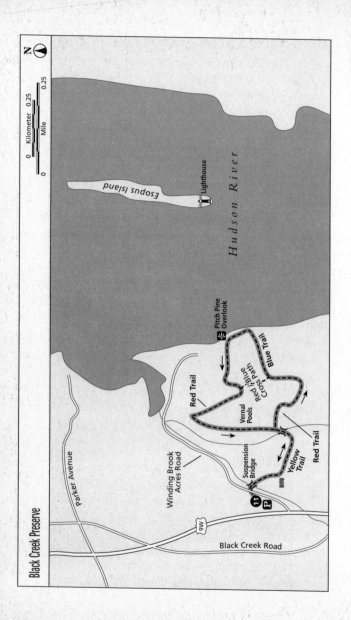

Black Creek Preserve

N

0   Kilometer   0.25
0   Mile   0.25

Parker Avenue

Winding Brook Acres Road

Red Trail

Vernal Pools

Red Cross Path
Blue Path

Blue Trail

Red Trail

Yellow Trail

Suspension Bridge

9W

Black Creek Road

Hudson River

Esopus Island

Lighthouse

Pitch Pine Overlook

you see many leafy trees: American hornbeam, red maple, northern red oak, and pignut hickory.

0.2 You'll be pleased to find the bench at the top of the hill. There's an interpretive display here about trees. When you're ready, continue to follow the yellow markers.

0.3 Cross a small bridge over the creek. There's an interpretive display here about deer exclosures, fencing that keeps deer from devouring the plants that grow on the forest floor. Turn right on the Red Trail (you'll see red plastic markers) and continue to the vernal pools.

0.7 Turn right here on the Blue Trail to the Hudson River. (You can also continue straight onto the cross path between the Red and Blue Trails and return to the parking area if you wish, but you will miss the river view.) Descend to the river on the Blue Trail.

0.8 Here is the Hudson River. There's usually a good breeze coming off the river here. Turn left and continue along the river for some great views.

0.9 This is Pitch Pine Overlook, the best vantage point from which to enjoy the river. There's a log bench here if you'd like to pause and contemplate the view. When you're ready, the trail continues behind you. Follow the Blue Trail and begin a gradual ascent.

1.0 The cross trail goes straight here. Turn right on the Red Trail, and continue through the vernal pools area. In spring, look for still pools of water that may host spring peepers and other frogs. Watch on the ground for spotted salamanders and other small amphibians.

1.4 Turn right on the Yellow Trail; this is the trail on which you arrived. After a short ascent, the trail is mostly downhill to the suspension bridge and back to the parking area.

1.8 You've reached the trailhead and the parking lot.

12 Pawling Nature Preserve

Take your first steps on the Appalachian Trail in this delicious little preserve, where the cool forest hides a waterfall and lots of tiny streams.

Distance: 2-mile loop
Approximate hiking time: 1 hour
Difficulty: Moderate
Trail surface: Dirt path
Best season: Apr–Nov
Other trail users: Appalachian Trail through-hikers
Canine compatibility: Pets not permitted
Fees and permits: Free
Schedule: Open daily sunrise to sunset
Maps: The Nature Conservancy, 195 New Karner Rd., Suite 200, Albany 12205; (518) 690-7850; www.nature.org
Water availability: None
Trail contact: The Nature Conservancy, 195 New Karner Rd., Suite 200, Albany 12205; (518) 690-7850; www.nature.org
Special considerations: Deer hunting is conducted here in season (usually mid-Nov through Dec). Wear orange if you hike then, or consider planning your hike for another time.

Finding the trailhead: From the south, take I-684 to its northern end in Brewster, and continue north on NY 22. Pass NY 55 and turn right on CR 68 (North Quaker Hill Road). Turn left on Quaker Lake Road. Continue 1.2 miles to the parking area. From the north, take I-84 south to the junction with I-684 and NY 22. Turn north on NY 22 and follow the directions above. GPS: N41 36.435' / W73 33.470.'

The Hike

Rescued by concerned neighbors and the Nature Conservancy from centuries of settlement, grazing, and logging, Pawling Nature Preserve now features hemlock and second-growth oak forests, healthy wetlands, and an impressively rocky gorge. The dominant feature, the 1,053-foot Hammersly Ridge, towers over the gorge and provides a vantage point for views of the adjacent Great Swamp—if you choose to climb to its summit.

This hike takes a different direction: We've traded major changes in elevation for the opportunity to hike a sliver of the Appalachian Trail, the granddaddy of the nation's National Scenic Trails. Whether you're a seasoned hiker or a casual walker, chances are you've dreamed of hiking some portion of this 2,175-mile-long footpath. There's no time like the present! This hike follows only about half a mile of the total length, but it's enough to show you the trail condition, familiarize you with the blazing system, and allow you to brag at parties about hiking part of "the AT."

As this relatively easy loop trail begins, you'll find the Duell Hollow Brook cascade tumbling (or trickling in summer) down the gorge's rocky sides. The up-and-down route gives you glimpses into a forest in which white-tailed deer are commonplace and chipmunks rule the understory. Wet spots in the woods attract six species of salamanders and five frog varieties. The Nature Conservancy works to preserve rare plants that grow here: devil's bit, scarlet Indian paintbrush, yellow wild flax, and more.

Miles and Directions

0.0 The trail begins to the right of the parking lot. Stop at the trail registry to sign in. You will follow the Yellow Trail (green plastic markers with yellow arrows and the Nature Conservancy oak-leaf logo) to begin this hike.

0.1 To your right, you can see the Duell Hollow Brook Creek waterfall cascading into the gorge. Take the side path to

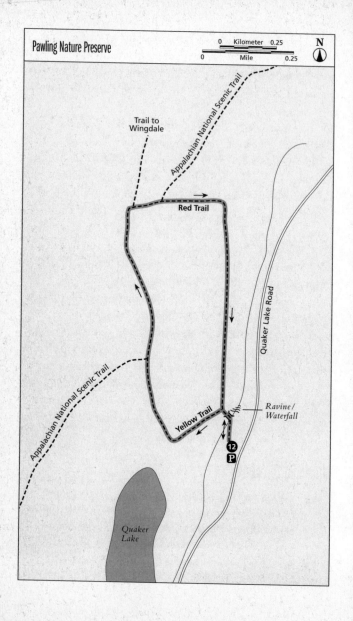

Pawling Nature Preserve

0   Kilometer   0.25
0   Mile   0.25

N

Trail to
Wingdale

Appalachian National Scenic Trail

Red Trail

Quaker Lake Road

Appalachian National Scenic Trail

Yellow Trail

Ravine/
Waterfall

12 P

Quaker
Lake

the falls for a closer look. (This may be a tiny trickle in a dry summer.) When you're ready, return to the trail and continue to follow the yellow markers straight ahead. Cross a bridge over the creek, and intersect with the Red Trail on your right. Bear left on the Yellow Trail.

0.4 Other trails go right and left here. Continue straight and then right on the Yellow Trail.

0.6 The Appalachian Trail (AT) enters from the left and joins the Yellow Trail. You'll see the white blazes and signs for the AT. From here, you're hiking on the AT for 0.7 mile.

0.9 A boardwalk goes left and right here on the Red Trail. Take the right leg, and follow the Red and White Trails together.

1.0 A sign here for the trail to Wingdale marks the beginning of the Green Trail. Continue straight on the combined Red and White Trails.

1.2 The AT goes left here, and the Red Trail goes right. Turn right and continue the loop. This concludes your hike on the Appalachian Trail.

1.4 The trail makes a sharp right (south). Cross two streams on large rocks.

1.7 Here's another stream to cross on mud and logs.

1.8 After another bridge, turn left on the yellow trail, and follow it back to the parking area.

2.0 You've reached the parking lot and your vehicle.

13 Walkway Over the Hudson State Historic Park and Loop Trail

Cross a railroad bridge high above the Hudson River, and cross back on the Mid-Hudson Bridge for some of the valley's most spectacular views.

Distance: 4.2-mile loop
Approximate hiking time: 2.5 hours
Difficulty: Moderate
Trail surface: Concrete, metal, and paved
Best season: Apr–Nov
Other trail users: Joggers, families with strollers, wheelchairs, cyclists, inline skaters
Canine compatibility: Dogs permitted on leash
Fees and permits: Free
Schedule: Open daily sunrise to sunset
Maps: Walkway Over the Hudson State Historic Park, www.walkway .org

Water availability: Refreshments and portable toilets available at concession stands at either end of the railroad bridge
Trail contact: New York State Office of Parks, Recreation, and Historic Preservation; (845) 834-2867; nysparks.state.ny.us/ parks/178/details.aspx
Special considerations: The concrete walkway can be very hot in summer, with little or no shade. If you bring your dog, bring a water bowl and water, and be ready to carry a small dog if the pavement becomes too hot. No skateboards are permitted.

Finding the trailhead: The parking area is at 60 Parker Avenue in Poughkeepsie. **Traveling south on US 9** from Hyde Park, turn left at the junction with NY 9G and follow 9G until it becomes Parker Avenue. The parking will appear on the left in about .02 mile. **Traveling north on US 9,** turn right on NY 55 in Poughkeepsie and take US 44/NY 55 north at Washington Street. Continue north on Washington to Parker Avenue, and turn right. The parking lot will appear on the left in about .02 mile. GPS: N41 42.749' / W73 55.585'

The Hike

If you only hike one trail in the Hudson River Valley, the Walkway Over the Hudson may be the one for you. Whether you choose to hike the entire loop or you simply walk out onto the former Poughkeepsie-Highland Railroad Bridge to take in the amazing river views, you will have no finer opportunity to appreciate the Hudson River and its beautiful valley than from this vantage point.

An inspired repurposing of an industrial bridge, the Walkway Over the Hudson puts back into use a nineteenth-century railroad bridge that served as a major rail corridor for many decades. When fire severely damaged the bridge in 1974, the old structure stood dormant until a group of enthusiastic citizens came together with state and federal governments to repair the bridge and transform it into a new state park.

The wide, smooth, modern walkway opened on October 3, 2009, and now stands as the longest elevated pedestrian bridge in the world. Visitors can stroll 212 feet above the river's surface and admire a spectacular view of the river to the north and south. A sunny summer Sunday can draw thousands of people to the park, making downtown Poughkeepsie a new meeting place for neighbors and friends throughout the Hudson River Valley.

Recognizing the value of a longer walk for energetic hikers, the state park has designated a loop trail route that crosses this bridge and the Mid-Hudson Bridge about half a mile south. A highly trafficked segment of US 44 and NY 55, the Mid-Hudson Bridge has a pedestrian walkway

Walkway Over the Hudson State Historic Park and Loop Trail

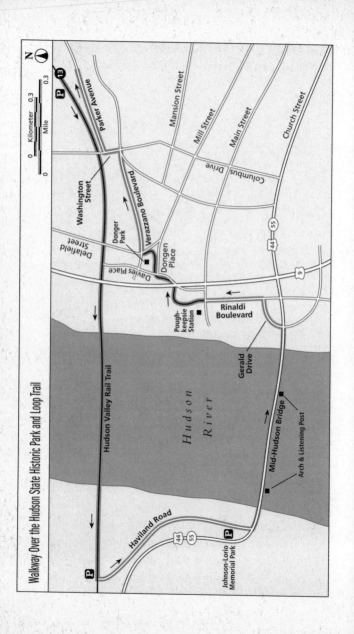

and an attraction of its own: Bridge Music, the remarkable accomplishment of composer Joseph Bertolozzi. The sounds of traffic crossing the bridge inspired Bertolozzi to write a series of pieces that can be described as percussive funk, created using only the sounds he could generate by making the bridge itself his drum kit. You can listen to a wide selection of these jazzy pieces when you reach the Mid-Hudson Bridge arches, where you will find speakers and buttons to push to hear Bertolozzi's Bridge Music.

Miles and Directions

0.0 From the parking area, the walkway leads west. Pass through shady woods and over a Poughkeepsie neighborhood before the bridge begins to cross the river. You'll find food concessions here. Once you're on the bridge, the walk across the bridge continues for 1.28 miles.

1.5 The bridge ends here. The walkway continues to your left (southwest) on a paved path. There's parking on this side of the bridge as well. Turn left at the end of the parking area, and continue to walk down the access road. US 44 and NY 55 are on your right.

2.1 At the end of the access road, you'll find Johnson-Iorio Memorial Park. There's a parking area here with interpretive signage about the Mid-Hudson Bridge. Turn left onto the bridge's pedestrian walkway. You're separated from the car traffic by guardrails and steel grating.

2.2 Here's the first Bridge Music listening post, on the first arch. You'll also see signs here about peregrine falcons nesting on this arch; if you're here between February and June, keep an eye out for peregrines flying around this post.

2.5 The second arch has another listening post. You're welcome to linger on the bridge, admire the view, and listen to the music for as long as you like.

2.8 At the end of the bridge, turn left on the walkway trail. The route will be obvious; the sidewalk is fenced here and descends to street level. When you reach Rinaldi Boulevard, turn left.

2.9 Turn right on Main Street. At this corner, there's a plaza with several restaurants, adjacent to Poughkeepsie Station's pedestrian walkway. You may want to stop here for lunch, ice cream, or a smoothie. When you're ready, continue to the covered pedestrian walkway and turn left onto the walkway. Continue into the station, and turn right. Pass the ticket counter and snack bar and come out on the east side of the station. Continue north on the sidewalk to Davies Place.

3.0 When you reach Dongen Park, turn right onto Dongen Place. Continue through the park to Mill Street.

3.3 Turn left on Mill Street, and continue to Verazzano Boulevard. Turn right on Verazzano.

3.4 Turn left on Washington Street.

3.8 Turn right on Parker Avenue. Continue on Parker to the parking area.

4.2 Here is the parking area.

14 Constitution Marsh Audubon Center and Sanctuary

Take an intimate look at a tidal marsh from the inside, surrounded by head-high vegetation, gently flowing water, and the songs of marsh-loving birds.

Distance: 1.1-mile lollipop
Approximate hiking time: 1 hour
Difficulty: Moderate
Trail surface: Dirt path and boardwalk
Best season: Apr–Nov
Other trail users: Hikers only
Canine compatibility: Pets not permitted
Fees and permits: Free
Schedule: Open daily 9:00 a.m.–6:00 p.m.
Maps: National Geographic Topo!, NY/NJ edition
Water availability: Restrooms inside the visitor center available Tuesday through Sunday, 9:00 a.m.–5:00 p.m. Hours are limited in winter.
Trail contact: Constitution Marsh Audubon Center and Sanctuary, 127 Warren Landing Rd. (physical address), Garrison 10524; mailing address is PO Box 174, Cold Spering, 10516, (845) 265-2601; www.constitution marsh.org
Special considerations: Sunscreen is critical; insect repellent is not.

Finding the trailhead: The sanctuary is on the east side of the Hudson River at 127 Warren Landing Road in Garrison. From I-87, take exit 17 toward I-84/Newburgh/Stewart Airport. Merge onto I-84 east and continue to the NY 9D exit. Turn right at the end of the ramp and follow 9D south to Indian Brook Road. Go slightly right and continue to the parking area at the intersection of Indian Brook Road and Warren Landing Road. GPS: N41 24.090' / W73 56.268'

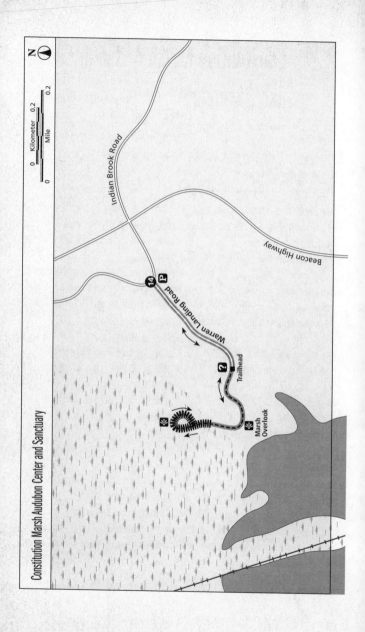

Constitution Marsh Audubon Center and Sanctuary

The Hike

It's one thing to stand on the edge of a marsh and peer into it to see what's going on there—but it's quite another to walk right into the tall grasses and reeds and become part of the action. The boardwalk at Constitution Marsh gives you exactly this opportunity, providing a dry, sturdy, remarkably unobtrusive route into the heart of this freshwater tidal marsh.

Your hike begins with a fairly quick descent from the parking area down a dirt road, bringing you to the visitor center with its interpretive displays and restrooms. Listen for Louisiana waterthrush here, one of the sanctuary's specialty birds. From here, follow the Blue Trail into the woods and up a challenging incline to a rewarding view of the marsh and the Hudson River beyond.

A quick descent brings you to the boardwalk, where the fun really begins: This gorgeous cattail marsh resonates with marsh wrens' chattering song, punctuated by calls of the occasional common yellowthroat or red-winged blackbird. Song sparrows pop up to the tops of the tall grasses, while Virginia rails skulk quietly at the edge of the reeds. A belted kingfisher may land on the boardwalk railing to check you out. Muskrat lodges—piles of sticks and mud—may be visible at the base of the cattails. Watch for these animals and for fish in the calm waters as you pause at the boardwalk's many viewing areas.

You'll return the way you came, through the woods and down the rocky paths. While this may not be the largest wildlife sanctuary in this book, it's a satisfying walk with more nature packed into a condensed area than many trails can show you over several miles.

Miles and Directions

0.0 From the parking area, walk downhill to the southwest until you reach the visitor center. The trailhead is past the visitor center on the edge of the woods.

0.3 Follow the blue diamond-shaped markers. The trail begins as a mowed grass path, but once you cross a small bridge, it changes to a dirt path through the woods. At the T intersection, bear left on the Blue Trail. Bear right at the next intersection.

0.4 The trail turns right and goes up a set of rock steps. Soon you reach an overlook point, where you can see the marsh through the maple and pine trees. Continue up the stone walkway and steps to the bench at the top of the hill. The view of the marsh and the Hudson River is worth a pause to catch your breath. From here, the trail descends to the boardwalk.

0.5 The boardwalk begins. Enter the tidal marsh, where high tide occurs every twelve and a half hours. The tide brings ocean fish up into the river, and they stop here to lay their eggs. If you're here in summer, watch for young fish in the open waters. The boardwalk forms a loop, with three viewing platforms and benches along its route.

0.6 You've completed the boardwalk loop. Return the way you came, on the straight section of boardwalk and over the hill to the visitor center.

0.8 Here is the visitor center. Turn northeast and walk up the road to the parking area.

1.1 You've returned to the parking lot.

15 Hunter Brook Preserve

A woodland ramble along a brook's edge offers a glimpse of a developed area's natural past.

Distance: 2.5-mile lollipop
Approximate hiking time: 1.5 hours
Difficulty: Easy
Trail surface: Dirt path
Best season: Apr–Nov
Other trail users: Hikers only
Canine compatibility: Dogs permitted on leash
Fees and permits: Free
Schedule: Open daily dawn to dusk

Maps: Westchester Land Trust, www.westchesterlandtrust.org/files/page%2057.pdf
Water availability: None
Trail contact: Westchester Land Trust, 403 Harris Rd., Bedford Hills 10507; (914) 241-6346; www.westchesterlandtrust.org
Special considerations: Watch for poison ivy and ticks.

Finding the trailhead: From the Taconic State Parkway, take US 202 west and turn left on Pine Grove Court. Take the immediate right onto Old Crompond Road. Continue on Old Crompond to Hunterbrook Road, and drive 1.1 miles to Fox Tail Lane. Park in the designated area on the right and walk to the trailhead. GPS: N41 16.485' / W73 50.335'

The Hike

When two land trusts—Westchester and Yorktown—and a developer work together to preserve a sliver of green space, the result can be as delightful as this little forty-five-acre park. Carefully marked, lightly maintained trails (originally established by Wilder-Balter Partners, the developer of the surrounding neighborhood) provide a sense of wilderness in the middle of a suburban subdivision, leading hikers into a mixed deciduous and conifer woods loaded with nut trees, ground flowers, singing birds, the occasional hopping amphibian, and small furry animals.

Hunter Brook itself runs the length of this park, carefully shielded by the surrounding undeveloped land. The brook is a tributary of Croton Reservoir, making it an important element in protecting the water supply for this part of Westchester County. It's also a lifeline for local animals and fish, including mink, muskrat, brook trout, and bluegills. The surrounding woods are home to barred and great horned owls, wood thrushes, warblers, vireos, catbirds, and many other bird species that nest and raise their young here.

Your hike follows the brook for a short way before breaking off to cross the woods, rejoining the brook again as the trail crosses a steel bridge. From here, a long, narrow loop gives you a thorough overview of the many different tree species that grace this park, finally returning to the bridge to escort you out along the entrance path.

Miles and Directions

0.0 Park your car and walk west on Fox Tail Lane to the trailhead. Enter the park on a mowed path through tall vegetation. This opens out to a shady, wide dirt path as it reaches Hunter Brook. Look for the white plastic Yorktown Parks Department trail markers with black printing, and follow these along the trail.

0.6 Cross two old stone walls. You'll begin to see Westchester Land Trust signs along the trail.

0.7 Cross a small wooden bridge, just before you come to the big steel bridge over Hunter Brook. As you arrive at the bridge, a trail comes in from the left. This is the trail to

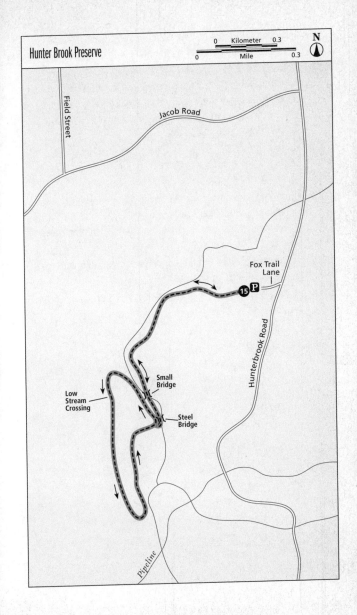

Hunter Brook Preserve

Field Street

Jacob Road

Fox Trail Lane

P 15

Hunterbrook Road

Small Bridge

Steel Bridge

Low Stream Crossing

Pipeline

N

0   Kilometer   0.3
0   Mile   0.3

Beekman Court, the second park entrance. Continue across the bridge, and bear right on the other side of the brook.

1.0 At the bend in the loop trail, you'll see green trail markers. Follow these as the trail goes up an incline. These mark the south-going leg of the loop. Cross a small stream on stones. When you see a large pile of rocks blocking a streambed, keep left and cross the stream.

1.1 Cross a stream that's low in a ditch. There's shagbark hickory in this area; you may see the nuts on the ground. Watch for tiny frogs.

1.4 Cross a stream on two logs. In about fifty steps, you'll cross another one. Soon you'll see the white markers as the green-marked trail ends. Turn left on the trail with the white markers.

1.8 You've arrived back at the bridge. Cross it and turn left on the trail on which you arrived.

2.5 Here is Fox Tail Lane. Your vehicle is down the road to the left.

16 Harriman State Park: Iron Mines Loop

Clear mountain lakes, forest-covered peaks, rocky outcroppings, and a summit with a spectacular view—it's all worth the extra effort Harriman demands.

Distance: 2.7-mile loop
Approximate hiking time: 1.5 hours
Difficulty: More challenging
Trail surface: Dirt path
Best season: Apr–Nov
Other trail users: Hikers only
Canine compatibility: Dogs permitted on leash, with muzzle
Fees and permits: Free
Schedule: Open daily dawn to dusk
Maps: Hiker's Marketplace, New York–New Jersey Trail Conference, 156 Ramapo Valley Rd., Mahwah, NJ 07430; (201) 512-9348; www.nynjtc.org/panel/goshopping
Water availability: None
Trail contact: Palisades Interstate Park Commission, Bear Mountain, 10911; (845) 786-2701; nysparks.state.ny.us/parks/145/details.aspx
Special considerations: Boots with ankle support are a must in this park.

Finding the trailhead: From I-87, take exit 15A (Sloatsburg). Turn left at the bottom of the ramp onto NY 17 north, and drive through Sloatsburg. Turn right at the first traffic light after the village onto Seven Lakes Drive. Continue on Seven Lakes Drive for 8 miles to the parking area for Lake Skannatati, on the left side of the road. (The parking area is 0.7 mile after the Kanawauke Circle.) GPS: N41 14.426' / W74 06.153'

The Hike

What does the quintessential downstate New York hike look like? Look no further than Harriman State Park, where this loop—a relatively easy hike compared to the rest of the park—takes you through areas of mixed forest, huge boulders, and exposed faces of granite and metamorphic gneiss. The payoff comes at the top of Pine Swamp Mountain, a low peak by Adirondack standards but with a sweeping view of the surrounding Hudson Highlands. You'll be glad you braved the vigorous ascent when you arrive at the top.

You may expect old-growth forest here, but most of the trees here are second growth, replanted after decades of iron mining stripped this area bare before and after the Civil War. The mines' furnaces required copious amounts of charcoal made from firewood, turning the forest into a continuous raw fuel source for iron ore processing. Mining stopped when Pennsylvania coal and Minnesota iron began to overshadow the Highlands' iron production at the turn of the twentieth century. That's when the Harriman family presented the state of New York with 30,000 acres of their private land adjacent to an existing park, turning this area into an outdoor paradise for hikers, campers, boaters, and many others.

While this hike takes you through the remains of some of these mines, they are not easy to spot—in part because the land has recovered so strongly from the mining days. Today the land appears as natural as it may have before the mines, the forests broken only by peaceful blue lakes and silver gray rock faces jutting through the thriving understory.

The first part of this hike follows the Long Path, a footpath from Altamont in the Albany area all the way to the George Washington Bridge in Fort Lee, New Jersey. Originally a project of the Mohawk Valley Hiking Club, this 347-mile trail crosses the Shawangunk and Catskill Mountains, winding through salt marshes at its southern end and climbing to 4,000 feet in the Catskills' boreal forests. It's only recently that the "parakeet aqua" blaze color has been used from one end of the trail to the other, but wherever you see this shade, you'll know you're on the Long Path.

Miles and Directions

0.0 Park at Lake Skannatati, and begin following the aqua blazes at the northwest corner of the lot. You'll see white blazes with a red inverted triangle here as well; this is the trail on which you will return to the lot at the end of your hike. Almost immediately, another path goes right; bear left along the edge of the lake and follow the aqua blazes.

0.2 Turn right on the aqua blazed path (the Long Path). (Another path goes left here.)

0.8 Cross a stream on large boulders. Begin a short ascent.

1.1 The Yellow Trail goes left and right here. Turn right on the Yellow Trail, and begin following a dirt road.

1.5 You're in a young hemlock woods. The pond to your right is the center of Pine Swamp. Look for remnants of Pine Swamp Mine ahead.

1.7 Reenter the woods here. Three yellow blazes on a tree signal the end of the Yellow Trail. Turn right and follow the white blazes with a red inverted triangle in the center. This is the Arden-Surebridge Trail (A-SB). Cross a stream on rocks (this may be a rushing cascade in spring). In about ten steps, there's a box canyon to your left. Explore if you wish, and continue on the A-SB trail when you're ready.

1.8 There's a cascade to your left; it may be dry in summer. In about 400 feet, you'll see a remnant of a stone wall. This is

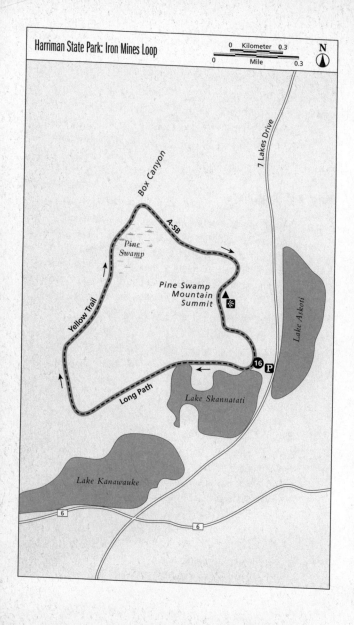

Harriman State Park: Iron Mines Loop

Box Canyon

A-SB

Pine Swamp

Yellow Trail

Pine Swamp Mountain Summit

Long Path

Lake Skannatati

16 P

Lake Askoti

7 Lakes Drive

Lake Kanawauke

6

6

N

Kilometer 0.3
0
Mile 0.3
0

all that remains of the area in which miners lived from the 1830s to the 1880s. The trail ascends steeply for a short stretch here, and then begins an up-and-down section on a rockier path.

1.9 Begin a gradual but challenging half-mile ascent to the top of Pine Swamp Mountain.

2.4 You've reached the summit of Pine Swamp Mountain at 1,165 feet. The view is obscured at this spot; continue to follow the trail to your left (south) for a better vantage point.

2.5 Here's the view you came to see. Lakes Skannatati and Askoti lie in front of you, and the forest-covered Catskill Mountains extend to the west, north, and south. You can see Seven Lakes Drive below, the only road that traverses this vista. When you're ready, follow the A-SB trail blazes downward to your left. The descent begins as a bit of a scramble over large boulders, but soon it becomes an easy, shady descent through the woods.

2.7 The trail ends at the parking area from which you began.

17 Old Croton Aqueduct Trail: Scarborough to Sleepy Hollow

Follow the course of New York City's original water source, on a shady trail through lush woodland with occasional dashes of history.

Distance: 3.6-mile shuttle or 7.2 miles out-and-back

Approximate hiking time: 1.5 hours one way, or 3 hours round trip

Difficulty: Easy

Trail surface: Dirt and mowed-grass path

Best season: Apr–Nov

Other trail users: Trail runners, cross-country skiers, cyclists, equestrians

Canine compatibility: Dogs permitted on leash

Fees and permits: Free

Schedule: Open daily sunrise to sunset

Maps: Available from Friends of the Old Croton Aqueduct Inc., (914) 693-4117, or for purchase at www.aqueduct.org

Water availability: At gas service stations along US 9

Trail contact: Old Croton Aqueduct State Historic Park, 15 Walnut St., Dobbs Ferry 10522; (914) 693-5259 or (914) 631-1470; nysparks.state.ny.us/parks/96/details.aspx

Finding the trailhead: From the north or south, take the Thruway (I-87 north) to exit 9 (Tarrytown/Sleepy Hollow/US 9 north). Travel north on US 9 for 4.6 miles to River Road in Briarcliff Manor. Turn left on River Road and immediately park in the parking area to the left of the road across from Scarborough School. GPS: N41 07.832' / W73 51.671.' **To reach the second parking area at the end of the hike,** from exit 9 on I-87, travel north on US 9 to Bedford Road in Sleepy Hollow. Turn right on Bedford Road and continue to the Old Croton

Aqueduct State Historic Park parking area. GPS: N41 05.212' / W73 51.35'

The Hike

One of the area's oldest and most established walking trails, the Old Croton Aqueduct Trail connects the Lower Hudson Valley with Yonkers and the Bronx by following the route of New York City's first transported water supply. Pedestrians, cyclists, and horseback riders now travel along the top of the aqueduct, an underground brick tunnel 8½ feet high and 7½ feet wide. Your hike takes you atop the protective covering of the earth that shields the aqueduct from the elements, allowing this remarkable feat of engineering to carry clean water from Croton Dam all the way to the center of New York, where it filled reservoirs on the sites of today's Great Lawn in Central Park and the New York Public Library.

Old Croton Aqueduct was retired in 1965 (although parts of it still bring water to Ossining), but its subterranean passageways still stand, descending just 13 inches per mile along the aqueduct's 41-mile length. The surface level served as an informal walkway for local and long-distance pedestrians throughout the aqueduct's history. Today, Old Croton Aqueduct State Historic Park provides excellent strolling, cycling, and hiking to tens of thousands of area residents each year.

This hike provides a sampling of the trail's numerous scenic and historical attributes. You'll pass three ventilators, cylindrical stone towers that allow fresh air to circulate over the water below. This trail segment crosses the Archville Bridge, which reconnected segments of the trail after a seventy-four-year severance. Perhaps best of all, you will pass through Sleepy Hollow—a real place after all—where author Washington Irving penned his classic tale of Ichabod Crane and the Headless Horseman. Irving's remains are interred in the Sleepy Hollow Cemetery (as are those of legendary industrialist and philanthropist Andrew Carnegie), a stop worthy of a detour from the main trail.

Miles and Directions

0.0 From the parking area on River Road in Scarborough, begin walking south on the aqueduct trail. The path is mowed here, with a narrow, bare, dirt trail running down the middle. There's a neighborhood just beyond the wooded area to your right.

0.2 Here is #10 ventilator.

0.4 Note the trail markers (the first you've seen) here. These are the State of New York Taconic Region markers, and are white plastic disks with black ink. The trail turns right here; you'll walk a short paved portion past a private home. Soon the trail bears left across this private property. Continue on the trail to Country Club Lane. Cross and continue straight on the trail.

0.8 A connecting trail goes right here. Bear left. The trail becomes a wide, crushed stone path through a lovely wooded area. You'll see many Asian wineberry bushes along the trail; these bear fruit in July. You're welcome to sample these.

0.9 This is the Archville Bridge. A stone marker here notes that the aqueduct's first arch over a road—Broadway in this case—was completed here in 1839. In a moment, you'll come to #11 ventilator.

1.8 A loop trail goes to the left here. Follow the green signposts for the "OCA" and turn right. Cross the bridge over NY 117. After the bridge, take the first trail to your right. You're now passing through Rockefeller State Park Preserve. Access to

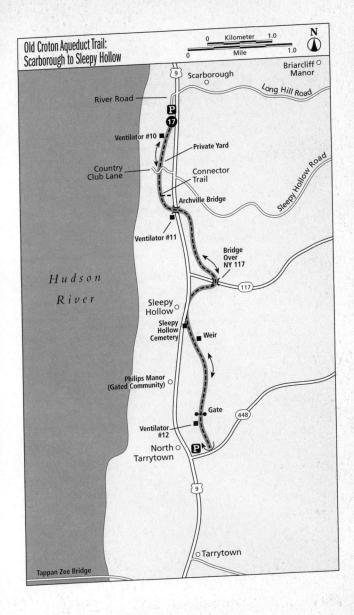

Old Croton Aqueduct Trail:
Scarborough to Sleepy Hollow

N

Kilometer
0   1.0
Mile
0   1.0

Briarcliff Manor

Scarborough

Long Hill Road

River Road

P
17

Ventilator #10

Private Yard

Country Club Lane

Connector Trail

Archville Bridge

Sleepy Hollow Road

Ventilator #11

Bridge Over NY 117

Hudson River

117

Sleepy Hollow

Sleepy Hollow Cemetery

Weir

Philips Manor (Gated Community)

Gate

448

Ventilator #12

North Tarrytown

P

9

Tarrytown

Tappan Zee Bridge

the preserve is free from here. You'll see short blue posts that indicate intersections between the preserve's 55 miles of carriage roads and the Old Croton Aqueduct Trail.

2.7 Another trail crosses the aqueduct trail. Continue straight. Sleepy Hollow Cemetery is on your right. In about fifty steps, you'll come to a weir, a large masonry edifice that contains a metal gate. When the aqueduct required maintenance, operators could lower the gate to divert the flow of water through the tunnel. Weirs were used at river crossings—the aqueduct crosses the Pocantico River here.

3.3 As you approach the wrought-iron gate ahead, the Hudson River and the Tappan Zee Bridge come into view on your right. Pass around the right side of the gate. The trail continues across the street.

3.4 Here is #12 ventilator.

3.6 Cross Bedford Road to the Old Croton Aqueduct State Historic Park parking area. If you are walking back to the beginning of the hike, this is your turnaround point. If you parked a car here, your hike has come to an end. You'll find many good places for lunch in Sleepy Hollow or just south in Tarrytown.

18 Mianus River Gorge Preserve

Walk where glacial melt created a rushing river, through one of the Hudson Valley's last remaining old-growth forests.

Distance: 1.6-mile loop
Approximate hiking time: 1 hour
Difficulty: Easy
Trail surface: Dirt path
Best season: Apr–Nov
Other trail users: Hikers only
Canine compatibility: No pets allowed
Fees and permits: Free
Schedule: Apr 1–Nov 30: Open daily 8:30 a.m.–5:00 p.m. Closed Dec 1–Mar 31

Maps: Available at interpretive kiosk at parking area, or at www .mianus.org/files/Trailmap.pdf
Water availability: Portable toilets at trailhead; no running water
Trail contact: Mianus River Gorge Preserve, Inc., 167 Mianus River Rd., Bedford 10506; (914) 234-3455; www.mianus.org
Special considerations: Insect repellent highly recommended; check for ticks after your hike.

Finding the trailhead: From I-684, take exit 4 for NY 172 (Bedford Road). Head east on NY 172 for 3.3 miles to Middle Patent Road, and turn right. Take the third left onto Millers Mill Road. Take the first right onto Mianus River Road. Turn left into the preserve parking lot. GPS: N41 11.100' / W73 37.243'

The Hike

This little gorge, the last remnant of the wild lands that existed here before the English arrived in 1683, became the catalyst for both private and federal preservation programs that protect natural landmarks across the United States. The Mianus River Gorge Preserve caught the attention of concerned citizens who made it the first land project of the Nature Conservancy in 1953. In 1964, the federal government designated the preserve as the first registered Natural Historic Landmark. Now the gorge is managed by the independent not-for-profit Mianus River Gorge Preserve, Inc.

What makes this gorge and forest so special? In an area congested with residential development, this gorge stands as a 764-acre respite from cleared landscapes and mowed lawns. Hidden from highway view by old-growth forest and by its own depth, the gorge shelters a sliver of wilderness that presents a cross-section of natural history. It formed 15,000 to 20,000 years ago when glaciers sliced through the region, and the river gorge continues to grow as its cascades wear away at the rock walls. The river, initially fueled by the melting Wisconsin glacier, now supplies water to more than 130,000 people in Westchester County, New York, and Fairfield County, Connecticut.

Your hike follows the river, descending to the water's edge and climbing back up the gorge's slopes through the woods. While we've chosen a loop trail, you can walk an additional ¾ mile to the end of the preserve, where Havermeyer Falls feeds the S. J. Bargh Reservoir during the wet seasons.

Miles and Directions

0.0 Follow the Red Trail, which begins to the left of the map kiosk. The well-maintained trail may be covered with wood chips; note the especially lush forest floor through here. The trail markers are wooden arrows with dots of color; continue to follow the Red Trail.

0.1 Here is the first river overlook. There's a bench here. From this point, the trail goes to the edge of the river, and descends a few steps to the riverbank, and then turns back up into the hemlock woods.

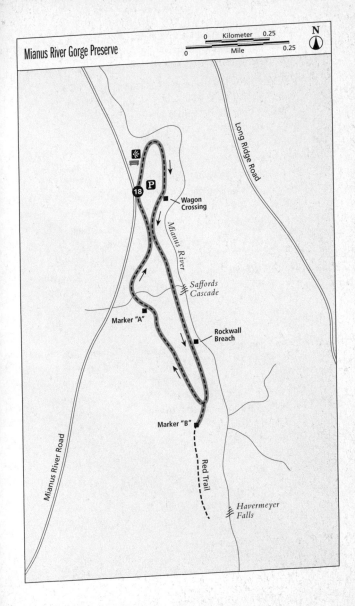

Mianus River Gorge Preserve

0   Kilometer   0.25

0   Mile   0.25

N

Long Ridge Road

Wagon
Crossing

Mianus River

Saffords
Cascade

Marker "A"

Rockwall
Breach

Marker "B"

Red Trail

Mianus River Road

Havermeyer
Falls

18
P

0.3 Here is marker #5 from the park brochure. You can see a narrow spot here at which horse-drawn wagons used to cross the river.

0.4 After an ascent, the Blue Trail goes right and left, while the Red goes left. Go left on the Red Trail. In a moment, the Green Trail goes left, while the Red and Blue Trails go straight. Go left on the Green Trail.

0.6 Here is Saffords Cascade, a stream that flows into the river over rocks. The ground vegetation around this stream gives the sense of a narrow wetland in the middle of a forest. Cross the cascade on big, flat rocks and begin an uphill stretch.

0.8 At the intersection with the Red Trail, turn left. Descend a little way and walk along the river to Rockwell Breach. This is the narrowest point in the gorge, where glacial waters cut the initial trench many millennia ago. From here, man-made soil and log steps take you up on the Red Trail. At the top of the steps, the trail follows a remarkably intact stone wall, a remnant of the settlements that were constructed on this land.

0.9 The Red and Blue Trails intersect here at Marker B. The Blue Trail is the return trail to the parking area. You are welcome to continue on the Red Trail another .75 mile to Havermeyer Falls and a view of the reservoir. If you prefer, turn north on the Blue Trail and start back toward the parking area. Begin to walk downhill.

1.2 The red and Blue Trails meet here once again, at Marker A. Bear left and continue on the combined Red/Blue Trail.

1.4 Here the Red, Green, and Blue Trails meet. Turn left on the Red and Blue Trails (the one marked RETURN on the wooden signs). Keep an eye out for American pipits, northern and Louisiana waterthrushes, and other puddle-loving birds in this wet area.

1.6 Here is the parking area.

Clubs and Trail Groups

Adirondack Mountain Club, Albany Chapter, P.O. Box 2116, ESP Sta., Albany 12220; (518) 899-2725; www.adk-albany.org; Mid-Hudson Chapter, P.O. Box 3674, Poughkeepsie 12603; www.midhudsonadk.org. The club offers a variety of hikes and programs to share the joy and knowledge of outdoor recreation.

Appalachian Mountain Club, Mohawk-Hudson Chapter; www.amcmohawkhudson.org. Formed to promote the protection and wise use of the Northeast's mountains, rivers, and trails, the club offers many outings and recreational opportunities throughout the year.

Catskill Mountain Club, P.O. Box 558, Pine Hill 12465. Outdoor recreational activities, volunteer stewardship of public resources, and environmental advocacy.

Hudson-Mohawk Bird Club, c/o Five Rivers Environmental Education Center, Game Farm Rd., Delmar 12054; www.hmbc.net. The club is devoted to field birding and the appreciation of wild birds through monthly programs, field trips, and its sanctuary in Schenectady.

Interstate Hiking Club, 33 Morris Ave, P.O. Box 52, Mt. Tabor, NJ 07878; www.interstatehikingclub.org. This club organizes hiking, canoeing, biking, snowshoeing, and maintenance trips on Friday, Saturday, and Sunday in northern New Jersey and southern New York.

Long Path North Hiking Club; www.schoharie-conservation
.org/memberclubs/lpn/index.html. Formed as an offshoot of
the New York/New Jersey Trail Conference, this organization maintains the Long Path and offers hikes on the trail in
every season.

New York–New Jersey Trail Conference, 156 Ramapo
Valley Rd., Mahwah, NJ 07430; (201) 512-9348; www
.nynjtc.org. The leading authority on trails in the New
York–New Jersey metropolitan region, the conference
works in partnership with parks to create and protect a network of more than 1,700 miles of trails.

Rip Van Winkle Hikers, 18 John St., Saugerties 12477;
(845) 246-8074; www.newyorkheritage.com/rvw/. This
club hosts year-round hikes in the Catskills and Mid-Hudson
for people of every skill level.

Sierra Club, Mid-Hudson Group, P.O. Box 1012, Poughkeepsie 12602; www.newyork.sierraclub.org/midhudson/.
The club offers weekly hiking or canoe trips for people
of all skill levels, as well as activities for national and local
conservation.

Westchester Trails Association, www.westhike.org. Hikes
and outdoor events are scheduled on Saturday and Sunday
throughout the year.

Additional Titles by Randi Minetor:

Backyard Birding: A Guide to Attracting and Identifying Birds
Best Easy Day Hikes Rochester, New York
Gettysburg: A Guided Tour Through History
Washington, D.C.: A Guided Tour Through History
Everglades National Park Pocket Guide
Gulf Islands National Seashore Pocket Guide
Best Easy Day Hikes Albany
Best Easy Day Hikes Buffalo
Best Easy Day Hikes Syracuse
Zion and Bryce Canyon National Parks Pocket Guide
Acadia National Park Pocket Guide
Great Smoky Mountains National Park Pocket Guide
New Orleans: A Guided Tour Through History
New York Immigrant Experience: A Guided Tour Through History
Fredericksburg: A Guided Tour Through History
Passport To Your National Parks® Companion Guide: National Capital Region
Passport To Your National Parks® Companion Guide: North Atlantic Region
Passport To Your National Parks® Companion Guide: Southeast Region

About the Author

Randi Minetor has written nineteen books to date for Globe Pequot Press (GPP), including the first three Passport To Your National Parks® Companion Guides and National Park Pocket Guides for the Great Smoky Mountains, Zion and Bryce Canyon, Acadia, and Everglades National Parks. She has also written a Pocket Guide for Gulf Islands National Seashore. Her GPP books include five in the Timeline Tours series: *Gettysburg; Washington, D.C.; Fredericksburg;* the *New York City Immigration Experience;* and *Historic New Orleans.* She has just completed work on a guide to backyard birding for Lyons Press. Her husband, Nic Minetor, is the photographer for her Pocket Guides, Timeline Tours books, and backyard birding book, and they have hiked in upstate New York for four other Best Easy Day Hikes guides to Rochester, Syracuse, Buffalo, and Albany, for which Nic is the cover photographer. Randi is also the National Parks Examiner on Examiner.com. She and Nic live in Rochester.

What's So Special about Unspoiled, Natural Places?

Beauty   Solitude   Wildness   Freedom   Quiet   Adventure
Serenity   Inspiration   Wonder   Excitement
Relaxation   Challenge

There's a lot to love about our treasured public lands, and the reasons are different for each of us. Whatever your reasons are, the national **Leave No Trace** education program will help you discover special outdoor places, enjoy them, and preserve them—today and for those who follow. By practicing and passing along these simple principles, you can help protect the special places you love from being loved to death.

The Principles of **Leave No Trace**

- 🐾 Plan ahead and prepare
- 🐾 Travel and camp on durable surfaces
- 🐾 Dispose of waste properly
- 🐾 Leave what you find
- 🐾 Minimize campfire impacts
- 🐾 Respect wildlife
- 🐾 Be considerate of other visitors

Leave No Trace is a national nonprofit organization dedicated to teaching responsible outdoor recreation skills and ethics to everyone who enjoys spending time outdoors.

To learn more or to become a member, please visit us at www.LNT.org or call (800) 332–4100.

Leave No Trace, P.O. Box 997, Boulder, CO 80306

AMERICAN HIKING SOCIETY

Because you **hike.**

We're with you every step of the way

American Hiking Society gives voice to the more than 75 million Americans who hike and is the only national organization that promotes and protects foot trails, the natural areas that surround them, and the hiking experience. Our work is inspiring and challenging, and is built on three pillars:

Volunteerism and Stewardship
We organize and coordinate nationally recognized programs—including Volunteer Vacations, National Trails Day ®, and the National Trails Fund— that help keep our trails open, safe, and enjoyable.

Policy and Advocacy
We work with Congress and federal agencies to ensure funding for trails, the preservation of natural areas, and the protection of the hiking experience.

Outreach and Education
We expand and support the national constituency of hikers through outreach and education as well as partnerships with other recreation and conservation organizations.

Join us in our efforts. Become an American Hiking Society member today!

American Hiking Society

1422 Fenwick Lane · Silver Spring, MD 20910 · (800) 972-8608
www.AmericanHiking.org · info@AmericanHiking.org